RADICAL CHRISTIAN DISCIPLESHIP

"Yoder consistently propels us to participate in Christ's mission of love in committed discipleship. Will we ever learn thoroughly to live by grace?"
—*Marva J. Dawn, theologian, speaker, author*

"The next time someone comes to me to learn more about Yoder and his work, this will be the first book I pull off the shelf. It is a readable and daring call for allegiance to the cross and deep transformation. A gift!"
—*Chris Lenschyn, associate pastor, Emmanuel Mennonite Church, Abbotsford, British Columbia*

"Here Yoder provides a series of concrete reflections on what his vision actually looks like. In doing so, his understanding of radical Christian discipleship is all the more radical. Nothing deserves to be called radical if it is somehow restricted only to a privileged few."
—*Chris K. Huebner, associate professor of theology and philosophy, Canadian Mennonite University*

"For too long the radical insight and practical wisdom of this pivotal Christian scholar and churchman have been unavailable to far too many Christians. *Radical Christian Discipleship* finally and ably fills a long-recognized void."
—*Philip D. Kenneson, professor of theology and philosophy, Milligan College*

"Yoder's provocative, profound thinking becomes available and understandable to the general reader in these short, readable essays."
—*Ronald J. Sider, president, Evangelicals for Social Action*

"Although these lectures, articles, and sermons were addressed to Mennonites in the 1950s and '60s, Yoder's underlying concern for 'living the cross' continues to echo prophetically for serious Christians in the twenty-first century."
—*Gayle Gerber Koontz, professor of theology and ethics, Anabaptist Mennonite Biblical Seminary*

"If you really want to know what someone thinks, overhear them talking to their family. This is Yoder speaking in prophetic voice primarily to his Mennonite family. Any group of disciples using this book as a source for conversation should plan on many late nights."
—*Mike Bowling, pastor, Englewood Christian Church, Indianapolis*

"These articles are every bit as relevant today as they were when Yoder first wrote them. Yoder's objectivity is striking—he seems unencumbered by the cultural assumptions that hinder the rest of us."
—*Shana Peachey Boshart, minister for Christian formation, Central Plains Mennonite Conference*

RADICAL CHRISTIAN DISCIPLESHIP

John Howard Yoder

Edited by John C. Nugent, Andy Alexis-Baker, and Branson L. Parler

Herald Press

Harrisonburg, Virginia
Waterloo, Ontario

Library of Congress Cataloging-in-Publication Data
Yoder, John Howard.
 Radical Christian discipleship / John Howard Yoder; edited by John
C. Nugent, Andy Alexis-Baker, and Branson L. Parler.
  p. cm.
 ISBN 978-0-8361-9666-5 (pbk. : alk. paper) 1. Christian life. I.
Nugent, John C., 1973– II. Alexis-Baker, Andy, 1975– III. Parler,
Branson L., 1980– IV. Title.
 BV4501.3.Y63 2012
 248.4—dc23
                                                            2012029035

Unless otherwise noted, Scripture text is quoted, with permission, from
the *New Revised Standard Version*, © 1989, Division of Christian
Education of the National Council of Churches of Christ in the United
States of America.

RADICAL CHRISTIAN DISCIPLESHIP
Copyright © 2012 by Herald Press, Harrisonburg, Virginia 22802
 Released simultaneously in Canada by Herald Press,
 Waterloo, Ontario N2L 6H7. All rights reserved.
Library of Congress Control Number: 2012029035
International Standard Book Number: 978-0-8361-9666-5
Printed in United States of America
Cover design by Brian Nugent, design by Joshua Byler
Cover photo by David Dean

16 15 14 13 12   10 9 8 7 6 5 4 3 2 1

To order or request information, please call 1-800-245-7894 in the
U.S. or 1-800-631-6535 in Canada. Or visit www.heraldpress.com.

Contents

Part Three: Conforming to Christ

Foreword

In recent years Malcolm Gladwell has popularized the notion of a "tipping point"—that moment when some new idea or movement builds up to the critical mass at which it outweighs its alternative and tips the scales, so to speak. What had been, up until now, simply a minority report—even a fringe resistance to the status quo—suddenly becomes not just a legitimate option but the obvious alternative. Everything changes. And we all wonder how anyone ever thought differently.

In the history of scientific thought, this phenomenon was first called a "paradigm shift" in the twentieth century. Philosopher Thomas Kuhn, who coined the phrase, pointed to Galileo as the prototypical martyr of the shift he was describing. Before Galileo, the official story was that we humans sat at the center of the universe—that the moon and the stars set their courses with reference to the Earth. How could it be otherwise? We were, after all, created a little lower than the angels—fashioned in God's very image.

When the telescope showed Galileo that earth was not at the center, Galileo's report was not warmly received. The data didn't compute. The intellectual world had not yet reached a "tipping point."

So goes the history of movements and ideas, says Kuhn and Gladwell. But they and others also point out that however momentous the sea change may seem when a Galileo comes along, a tipping point does not come from nowhere. Every paradigm shift has its eccentrics who always pointed to inconsistencies in the dominant way of naming things. Every tipping point has its time of building to a point of crisis. Before the Christ, after whom we count time differently, there is a voice crying out in the wilderness, "Prepare the way of the Lord!"

All of this matters because we are living on the cusp of a tipping point. This dizzying phenomenon is suggested whenever we read the newspapers (what few still remain) or watch the evening news (the varieties of which are so diverse that it can be difficult to imagine they are reporting the same reality). It is named much more clearly by our wisest social critics, those writers and poets who point out that we are witnessing the disintegration of established forms of government, economy, education, community, and family, while at the same time the earth cries out—indeed, while the data tells us that this planet is not the same place as where we were born. It has been unalterably changed by unprecedented global climate change.

It is no small surprise that the church is changing, too. Having wed itself to Christendom some 1700 years ago, Christianity is not just going through a midlife crisis. It is, quite literally, being born again. To many, this has felt like death for quite some time. It has been lamented by bishops who aren't sure how to make the payroll next month. It has been mourned by grandmothers who weep that their grandchildren do not have a church to anchor their lives in the way that they did when they were young—in a way that they now understand was crucial to their survival.

But on the other side of this painful dying, more and more people are beginning to celebrate signs of new life. It's a new dawn for the Christian movement. It's an exciting time to be alive. The way of life that Jesus taught and practiced has, in fact, reached something of a tipping point. We are living in the midst of a Great Awakening—what I like to call the "everyday awakening" of hope.

If this is the case—and I believe with all my heart that it is—we have not come here on our own. For some time now, there have been voices crying out in the wilderness, crazy folk for whom the data would never quite compute. In the light of this new dawn, we can see that they were, in fact, voices sent to us from beyond. As I look at the landscape of North American theology in the past century, few of those voices were more significant than that of John Howard Yoder.

I was introduced to Yoder in college via his classic text *The Politics of Jesus*. As a Southern Baptist kid who was trying to recover from the ambitions of the Religious Right, Yoder's vision of who Jesus was and how his movement challenged every human political option captured my imagination. Here was the "third way" I'd been longing for. But it wasn't an easy read. A real scholar, Yoder forced me to pay attention in history and biblical studies classes—even in sociology, philosophy, and psychology. He was engaging a dozen conversations that had their own language in the academy. While he could be crystal clear, he wasn't dumbing anything down.

When, several years later, I studied with Stanley Hauerwas at Duke Divinity School, this man who had spent his life in the academy told me he had known a lot of smart people, but there were only two he'd known whom he considered super-minds, operating on another level from the rest of us. One of them was the philosopher I was trying to understand at the time. The other was John Howard Yoder.

Our Einsteins, Newtons, Aristotles, and Platos are a gift to the world, but the energy of their minds is almost always claimed, in one way or another, by the economic and political interests of their day. (If not, as Plato taught a long line of intellectuals who have followed him, there is a price to pay.) But not so with John Howard Yoder. As it happened, Yoder was born into a stream of the Radical Reformation that had for hundreds of years practiced a resistance to the status quo—a protest that was rooted in a firm allegiance to Jesus. Yoder grew up in this Anabaptist faith. More important than his incredible mental acuity was the fact that his heart, mind, soul, and strength were claimed by Jesus.

And so the Anabaptist movement—a stream that has for some time been preparing us for post-Constantinian Christianity—gained one of the twentieth century's sharpest minds. In him, Christianity was given a seer who could look ahead to the awakening that we are only now beginning to experience on a broad scale. The world gained a witness who was able to be this precise in 1954: "When we preach the Christian gospel we are not talking about ideas; we are reporting events."

The great gift of the collection you are now holding—early talks and writings of Yoder, from which I've just quoted—is that they present Yoder's vision in some of the most accessible language I have ever read. They do so because they assumed an audience who were very much like me when I first read *The Politics of Jesus*—eager to understand but not well versed in the precise vocabularies of the academy. So, while these essays are every bit as smart as anything he ever wrote, they are popular in the truest sense: they seek to communicate as clearly as possible to everyday people the news that they report.

This news is *gospel*—good news in its truest and deepest sense. It is the hope that breaks in with power at just the moment when we realize that all our ways of finding health and wholeness in this world as we know it are dead ends. "The kingdom of God is at hand," Jesus announced. And, as Yoder says so well, it's not like a taxi whose departure depends on you hailing it. It's like a train of the old spirituals—that freedom train that's a-comin' whether we want it to or not. But it's comin' to save us. It's comin' to set us free. Once you've heard the song and seen its truth, you know that the only thing to do is get on board.

—*Jonathan Wilson-Hartgrove*
Ordinary Time, 2012

Acknowledgements

People who edit books are usually supported by a network of others who have made their work possible. When three editors are involved, that network grows considerably. This is especially so when none of the original essays were available in digital form. This meant that articles and booklets needed to be scanned and proofed for accuracy, and audio tapes had to be converted to digital form and then transcribed.

We are first of all grateful to Yoder's daughter, Martha Yoder Maust, for encouraging this project and granting us permission to make her father's work available to a wider audience. Mark Thiessen Nation was also instrumental in helping us envision what this three-volume project might look like. We also appreciate the patience of our spouses— Beth Nugent, Nekeisha Alexis-Baker, and Sarah Parler—as we constantly pored over this material when we may otherwise have been spending quality time with them.

We are grateful to Anne Meyer Byler, the reference librarian at Goshen College, Karl Stutzman, the digital services librarian at Anabaptist Mennonite Biblical Seminary, and James Orme, the head librarian at Great Lakes Christian College, for helping us locate copies of the material now contained in this collection.

It is somewhat challenging for a group of Yoder scholars like Andy, Branson, and John to identify various phrases and concepts in Yoder's writings that might be difficult for non-academics to understand. We are therefore deeply indebted to Mike Bowling, Chris Lenschyn, Sharon Peachey Boshart, Nekeisha Alexis-Baker, Ted Troxell, Mike Nugent, and James Wetzel for reading the manuscript and highlighting several sentences we missed that needed to be adjusted for the sake of clarity and ease of reading.

John Nugent and Branson Parler are pleased to thank their teaching assistants who aided their work on this project in a variety of ways. Aaron Woods and Joey Whittaker from Great Lakes Christian College assisted John. Melissa Martin Sells and Philip VanderWindt from Kuyper College assisted Branson. We are also grateful to Heather Bunce and Natasha Smith for giving the text a final round of proofreading before we sent it off to print. Their fresh eyes helped identify several minor errors that remained, though the astute reader will likely find more.

We are all grateful to Jonathan Wilson-Hartgrove for writing such a thoughtful foreword and to the pleasant staff at Herald Press for embracing this three-volume project. It is always difficult for publishers to decide if a particular volume will sell enough copies to make it worth their while to print. We were therefore thrilled to hear how excited Herald Press was to accept our proposal for a three-volume series and to allow John's brother, Brian Nugent, to work on the cover design. Finding an attractive and effective design concept that spans three volumes is no easy task, and Brian is to be commended for coming up with so many interesting possibilities.

Finally, we are all grateful to the many students, friends, and family members—too many to name here—who grew weary of learning from Yoder secondhand and challenged us to make his most stimulating ideas available in a form that nonacademics can read and comprehend. This book is for you!

Introduction

Christianity has an image problem. Prominent examples of Christians failing to follow Jesus are easy to come by and popular media has done much to exploit them. *Saturday Night Live* graphically illustrates this trend in a spoof of *VeggieTales*, a popular Christian cartoon series. We will spare you the details, but imagine Bob the Tomato, Larry the Cucumber, and company—now called the *Religetables*—reading pornographic material, killing infidels during the crusades, hanging innocent witches in Salem, damning people to hell, molesting young children, and brutalizing the masses during Armageddon, all while singing pious religious songs with their cute veggie voices. With our poor track record and even worse media exposure, it is no wonder that we Christians are often considered hypocritical, judgmental, self-centered, too political, and more focused on making converts than genuinely ministering to people.[1] This picture is not pretty.

Is the church nothing more than a self-righteous, self-enclosed lobbying group? Do we combine legalistic judgment with hypocritical lack of self-awareness? Is this why

---

1. See David Kinnaman and Gabe Lyons, *UnChristian: What a New Generation Really Thinks about Christianity . . . and Why It Matters* (Grand Rapids, MI: Baker, 2007).

so many people put up emotional and intellectual barriers to Christianity? Some Christians might dismiss such questions by pointing to Jesus' warning that the world will hate his followers (John 15:18). It is certainly true that the cross of Christ is scandalous to the world (1 Corinthians 1:18-25), but it is equally true that Jesus brought good news. Clearly, not all who hear the gospel as bad news do so simply because they are hard-hearted sinners. The problem goes much deeper. Those whom Christ has called to radical Christian discipleship are acting unchristianly. That is not just a problem of image. It is also a deeper problem of substance.

This is why John Howard Yoder's challenge to the church continues to be relevant today. Yoder's writings, which span from 1949 to his death in 1997, speak directly to the world's negative assessment of today's churches. Where churches have become self-focused and sheltered, Yoder calls us to be creative and mission-minded. He also challenges us to witness to Christ in every aspect of our lives. Where churches have become judgmental, Yoder calls us to be truly evangelistic, proclaiming the *good* news of God's offer of abundant life. Where churches have become conversion-focused, Yoder calls us to be disciple-focused, being and making followers of the way of Jesus. Where churches have become too political, Yoder calls for a new kind of politics in the body of Christ, embracing forgiveness instead of finger pointing, conflict resolution instead of polarized partisanship, and unity in Christ instead of competing special interest groups. Finally, where churches have become hypocritical, Yoder calls us to radical Christian discipleship, shunning legalism and self-righteousness and relying on the power of the Holy Spirit as we take up our cross and follow Jesus. Yoder's challenge to the church not only addresses surface issues of image, but tackles core issues of substance. He helps us ask again, Who is Jesus? And who are we called to be as his followers?

Who is John Howard Yoder?

At this point, you may be wondering, "Who exactly is John Howard Yoder?" A household name among some circles, Yoder is virtually unknown in others. For example, his most famous book, *The Politics of Jesus*, was named among the top ten books of the twentieth century by *Christianity Today*. Yet, if you were to poll the average Protestant, Catholic, or Orthodox congregation, Yoder would be far lesser known than other names in the top ten, including C. S. Lewis, Dietrich Bonhoeffer, J. R. R. Tolkien, Richard Foster, and Dorothy Day. Although the more academically inclined contributors to *Christianity Today* hold Yoder in high esteem, the average person in the pew has no idea who he is. We can begin to understand Yoder if we look at core commitments that characterized his life and work.[2] These core commitments can help explain why Yoder resonates with Christians of all traditions.

In his writing, Yoder is committed to reading and studying Scripture as the foundation of Christian life. Though he often uses historical and linguistic tools to illuminate specific texts and their context, Yoder never forgets that engaging Scripture is not merely an intellectual exercise but an activity that demands our obedience. Practical questions—not just theoretical or intellectual ones—run as an undercurrent in Yoder's work. Rather than argue about how to characterize the authority of Scripture or whether certain events really happened, he simply assumes that Scripture is authoritative and that the accounts we have are the ones God calls us to live by. Yoder stands out among theologians and ethicists of his time and ours for his commitment to basing his claims upon the entirety of Scripture, from Genesis to Revelation.[3]

Yoder is equally committed to the centrality of Jesus. The written Word ultimately points to the living Word by whom all things were created and in whom all things hold together.

---

2. For those interested in further biographical information, see Mark Thiessen Nation, *John Howard Yoder: Mennonite Patience, Evangelical Witness, Catholic Convictions* (Grand Rapids, MI: Eerdmans, 2006), and Earl Zimmerman, *Practicing the Politics of Jesus: The Origin and Significance of John Howard Yoder's Social Ethics* (Telford, PA: Cascadia / Scottdale, PA: Herald Press, 2007). For a helpful summary of key themes in Yoder's work, see Craig A. Carter, *The Politics of the Cross: The Theology and Social Ethics of John Howard Yoder* (Grand Rapids, MI: Brazos, 2001).

3. For an introduction to Yoder's interpretation of Scripture, see John C. Nugent, *The Politics of Yahweh: John Howard Yoder, the Old Testament, and the People of God* (Eugene, OR: Cascade Books, 2011).

As truly divine and truly human, Jesus reveals both who God is and who we are called to be. For Yoder, Jesus is unique, but this uniqueness does not hinder our ability to follow him. It enables us to do so by giving us a concrete example to follow. When Jesus comes as a servant, he calls us to take up the basin and towel and serve others. When Jesus comes to bear his cross, he calls us to take up our cross and follow him. When Jesus comes to show God's love to those who were enemies of God, he calls us to love our enemies as well. For Yoder, Jesus is not only central to Scripture, doctrine, and ethics, but also to world history. He challenges all who share that conviction to integrate it more consistently into all their thoughts and actions.[4]

Yoder was committed to his own Mennonite heritage. Born in 1927 and raised in the Mennonite church, he graduated from Goshen College in 1947. From 1949 to 1957, Yoder spent time in France, where he supervised two homes for children, engaged in numerous church unity meetings, oversaw the Mennonite Board of Missions and Charities relief program in Algeria, and pursued graduate education. When he returned to North America, Yoder served in numerous official capacities in Mennonite institutions. He served as a liaison between Mennonites and other denominational institutions such as the World Council of Churches. He also taught at Associated Mennonite Biblical Seminaries—recently renamed Anabaptist Mennonite Biblical Seminary, the name we use in this book— and in 1977 began teaching full time at the University of Notre Dame where he contributed to the Joan B. Kroc Institute for International Peace Studies until his death in 1997. Though Yoder stood within the Mennonite tradition, he also creatively reworked it in various ways. This made him a compelling figure well beyond his own tradition.[5] For example, he linked moral purity and mission in ways that were not so common; he emphasized strong continuity between the Old and New Testaments for understanding the nature and mission of the

---

4. Branson Parler unpacks Yoder's view of how all things hold together in Christ in *Things Hold Together: John Howard Yoder's Trinitarian Theology of Culture* (Harrisonburg, VA: Herald Press, 2012).

5. Nation, *John Howard Yoder*, 29.

church; he challenged believers not to be different from the world for the sake of difference but to be more like Christ; and he emphasized the sacramental dimensions of church practices in ways that bridge the gap between high church and low church views of them.

Yoder was also committed to church unity, which included helping others more faithfully live out their own heritage.[6] He intentionally met people on their own turf in order to call all Christians to be more faithful to Jesus. He did not call Calvinists, Catholics, or Campbellites to simply become Mennonite. He pointed to resources within those traditions that would make them more faithful to Scripture and to Christ. A prime example is Yoder's interaction with proponents of the just war tradition. While at Notre Dame, Yoder taught a graduate course on this subject to those who were training to become officers in the armed forces. As a pacifist, Yoder could have ignored or denounced adherents to just war theory, but he didn't. Through detailed and careful interaction, he took their heritage seriously and called them to do so as well. Yoder engaged evangelicals with the same rigor. As a result, when *The Christian Century* published an article on "The Year of the Evangelicals" in 1989, Yoder was pictured on the front cover along with figures as prominent as Billy Graham and Francis Schaeffer. Yoder's impact beyond Mennonite circles is evident in that three of the four editors involved in this series, Yoder's Challenge to the Church, come from beyond Mennonite circles.[7]

Finally, Yoder was deeply committed to mission. He even claimed that a church that is not missional is no church at all.[8] Yoder lived this out in his own life. He not only taught

---

6. For detailed treatment of Yoder's approach to church unity, see John C. Nugent, ed., *Radical Ecumenicity: Pursuing Unity and Continuity after John Howard Yoder* (Abilene, TX: Abilene Christian University Press, 2010). This collection contains an essay by Yoder on unity and a wonderful essay by Gayle Gerber Koontz about how Yoder lived out his pursuit of unity.

7. Influenced by Yoder's thought, Andy Alexis-Baker first joined a Mennonite church in 2000, but Branson Parler is Reformed, and John Nugent and Kate A. Kissling-Blakely (who will be involved in volume 3) are both part of the Christian Churches/Churches of Christ.

8. See John Howard Yoder, *Theology of Missions*, edited by Gayle

missions courses, but was deeply influential in shaping North American Mennonite mission in places like West Africa. An example might illustrate his viewpoint. Most missionary agencies in West Africa during the 1960s were trying to convert Africans involved in a movement called African-Initiated Churches (AICs). Yoder, by contrast, argued that converting people to the Mennonite church would stifle a genuine West African movement and would perpetuate European divisions in new places. In a brilliant stroke of guidance, he noted a strand of AICs that had begun as pacifist churches and urged missionaries to offer peace workshops to help strengthen that position, instead of convincing them to become Mennonites. In this way, Mennonites could participate in an organic discipleship process alongside other Christians without being anxious about their own denominational numbers.[9] Thus discipleship has a particular missional character, as Yoder expresses in chapter 17 of this volume. Far from remaining inwardly focused, the church is pushed out beyond itself through the Holy Spirit.

Challenge to the Church series

Although Yoder's voice continues to resonate across the landscape of academic Christianity, his challenge to the church seldom falls within earshot of today's average Christian. This is partly because most of his published works were directed toward scholars. Yet on many occasions Yoder addressed ordinary Christians, whether in local congregations, college chapels, or retreat centers. Unfortunately most of this material has not been published or was published in magazines that were not read widely beyond Mennonites. As editors of this series, we have collected, transcribed, and published this material because we believe Yoder's challenge to follow Jesus in all things still needs to be heard outside of academia.

Gerber Koontz and Andy Alexis-Baker (Downers Grove, IL: IVP Academic, 2013), forthcoming.

9. For a more detailed picture of Yoder's work in West African missions see David Shenk, "John Howard Yoder, Strategist for Mission with African-Initiated Churches," in *Missions from the Margins*, edited by James R. Krabill (Harrisonburg, VA: Herald Press, 2012).

This project began as one book that focuses on the topic of nonconformity (now volume 1). We then discovered a wealth of unpublished popular-level material scattered about in church audio collections, college libraries, and Yoder's personal archives. As we surveyed this material, it became clear that it fell into three thematic clusters that were ideally suited for a three-volume series. This first volume, *Radical Christian Discipleship*, concentrates on how individual Christians are called to follow Jesus completely in every aspect of our lives. This volume is introduced in greater detail below.

Volume 2, *Revolutionary Christian Citizenship*, will be published in 2013. It focuses on how Christians should relate to the nations in which they live. Yoder challenges churches to think about how they can be collective witnesses to the state and how individual believers can be witnesses in their everyday lives and practices. Building off the political nature of Jesus' ministry, this volume addresses how Christians should think about broad concepts such as power, enemy love, and Christian witness to the state. It also delves into specific issues such as voting, taxation, and peace.

Volume 3, *Real Christian Fellowship*, will be published in 2014. It focuses on how members of Christ's body ought to relate to one another as a community. It deals with core Christian practices including baptism, communion, making decisions, admonishing one another, serving the poor, singing songs, and curtailing practices that deny women full dignity in Christ. This volume is of particular value because Yoder recovers important biblical dimensions of these practices that have been lost over time. Whether one is part of a small rural congregation or a large city church, this collection will breathe fresh air into the everyday life of the body of Christ.

Radical Christian discipleship

This present volume focuses on discipleship. It is divided into three sections. The first section includes five lectures that Yoder gave at Goshen College in 1963. These lectures were part of an annual series that concentrated on nonconformity to the world. In typical fashion, Yoder reframes this issue by pointing out that the key to Christian obedience is not *non*conformity, but *conformity to Jesus*. Our mission is not to be different from the world, but to be similar to Christ. At the time of these lectures, Yoder was working full time as an administrative assistant for overseas mission with the Mennonite Board of Missions while also serving as a part-time instructor at the Mennonite Biblical Seminary in Elkhart, Indiana.[10]

Section 2 includes twelve articles, one which appeared in the *Gospel Herald* in 1954 and eleven which appeared in *Christian Living* magazine from 1955 to 1956.[11] The readers of *Christian Living* would have been members of the Mennonite Church, the branch of Mennonite faith from which Yoder came.[12] Congregations often subscribed to *Christian Living* and placed a copy in the church mailbox of each member. In these essays, Yoder deals with a variety of topics, including the Christian's relationship to money, time, truth, self-assertion, freedom, enemies, suffering, and history. Those who have been led to think of Mennonites as "against culture" will be surprised that Yoder asks not how we can avoid the world, but how Christ has freed us for service to the world.

The historical context of section 2 is especially important. Yoder is writing from Europe less than a decade after World War II and while the French-Algerian War was still being waged. As Yoder continued his studies and work in Europe, he wrote to North American Mennonites to call them to a vision of Christianity that was more radical and self-critical than what they were used to.[13] This meant asking hard questions not just about war and peace, but also about everything from middle-class economic stability to individualism, work, vacation, and rest. To those tempted to settle

---

10. Nation, *John Howard Yoder*, 21–22. Mennonite Biblical Seminary later merged with Goshen Biblical Seminary to form Associated Mennonite Biblical Seminaries, now renamed Anabaptist Mennonite Biblical Seminary.

11. Though these essays were written earlier than section 1, we place them second because they go into greater detail on some of the issues that are introduced in the first section.

12. For those unfamiliar with the Mennonite tradition, the General Conference Mennonite Church and the Mennonite Church have since merged to form Mennonite Church USA.

13. Yoder, "1980 Autobiography," quoted in Nation, *John Howard Yoder*, 20.

into comfortable accommodation to the emerging post-war North American culture, Yoder issues a powerful challenge to radical Christian discipleship.

The final section includes three sermons ranging from 1968 to 1978, a commencement address from 1963, and an article originally published in *Christian Ministry* magazine in 1955. Of particular historical interest is a sermon he delivered on the day after Martin Luther King Jr. was assassinated. These essays round out this collection by answering specific questions about discipleship that are raised in parts 1 and 2. What exactly is the cross that disciples have been called to take up? What does it mean to count the costs before following Jesus? Is it appropriate to soften the hard edges of the gospel for the sake of evangelism? What might radical Christian discipleship look like in the life of a specific community? What is God's role in our efforts to follow him in all things? The emphasis on peace, community, and mission in this final section anticipate, in many ways, the themes Yoder develops more fully in volumes 2 and 3 of this series.

Finally, we should say a word about our choice of the term *radical* in the title of this book. By "radical" we do not mean that what Yoder sets forth in these pages is only for a few far-left or far-right Christians who want to make disciples of themselves. Nor by "radical" do we mean that only a minority of Christians are called to this kind of discipleship. It is true that Yoder doesn't give us a flashy program by which to usher ever greater numbers into our ranks. Yet he preached and taught to anybody who would listen, and the vision set forth here is meant to propel Christians of all stripes into a deeper commitment to Christ and their neighbors (even enemy neighbors). Radicalness is thus for every Christian. One meaning of the term *radical* is "root" in the sense of origins. At the root of Christianity is Christ and at the root of what we proclaim about Christ is the cross and resurrection. What readers will find here is a root vision of what the cross and resurrection mean for Christian life.

Editorial concerns

Because all of these essays are historically situated, readers should not be surprised to see Yoder engage communism, the

USSR, the civil rights movement, France and Algeria, events from World War II, Fidel Castro, Nikita Khrushchev, and other headliners at the time he was writing. Sometimes the editors have furnished a footnote or worked a brief explanation into the text to situate the reference. Still, readers are encouraged to exercise their imaginations and to draw parallels from earlier decades to the issues facing Christians today. These essays are striking because, rather than being time-bound, they transcend the times and places in which they were written. As Christians face the perennial issues and questions of discipleship, Yoder's challenge to the church is just as relevant today as it was over fifty years ago.

Since our goal is to make Yoder's work available in an accessible format, we have edited his writings as necessary to help them read easier. We have not made changes that would compromise the substance of the original sermons or essays. Yoder himself acknowledged his limitations as a writer. In an unpublished letter he notes, "Clarity not being, by the way, the most evident virtue of my writing." A grammarian might observe that even this quote could benefit from revision for the sake of readability. Whether it was the effect of having such a rigorous and logical mind or the result of writing his dissertation in German, Yoder often constructed sentences in less-than-ideal ways. So we have sometimes changed word order, condensed a sentence where Yoder had been unduly wordy, adjusted punctuation, or added a word that helps improve the flow of a sentence. We have also conformed Yoder's language to contemporary gender-inclusive standards as was his own practice later in life. Scripture quotations have been converted to the NRSV, except where the original version makes a difference, in which case we identify the other translations in parentheses. Given the nature of these writings, there were few footnotes in the originals. All footnotes were therefore inserted by the editors, except when indicated otherwise.

In this three-volume series, we point to Yoder not as an end in himself, but as a herald. Yoder's challenge to the church reminds one of the voice that once cried in the Judean wilderness. In his call for Christians to follow Jesus, Yoder follows in the steps of John the Baptist who "was not the light," but who "came only as a witness to the light" (John

1:8). As we seek a life of radical Christian discipleship, may God's grace enable us to be witnesses to this same light.

—John C. Nugent
Andy Alexis-Baker
Branson L. Parler

Part One

Beyond Conformity

1

A Choice of Slaveries[1]

You are doomed to conformity. To be human is to be destined
to conform to some pattern, some example. The apostle Paul
says of Christians, "those whom he foreknew he also predes-
tined to be conformed to the image of his Son, in order that
he might be the firstborn within a large family" (Romans
8:29). The apostle had no better definition of what it means
to be a Christian than to speak of himself as a man who no
longer lives, but in whom Christ dwells. It is therefore not
new information, not a statement we did not know before,
when in 1 John we read, "As he is, so are we in this world"
(1 John 4:17). It could be said even more briefly: "We are he
in the world."

The goal of this sermon series is to remind ourselves how
Christians are called to be different from those things in the
world that are different from Christ. We must also remember
that the key to Christian obedience is not *non*conformity but
conformity. These themes lead us to the beginning of Romans
12. Here Paul pleads with his readers not to be conformed.
This theme of differentness is touched upon only in passing.
It is the prelude to a chapter that otherwise focuses on what

---

1. This is the first of five lectures that Yoder gave at Goshen College
in 1963. For more information see the introduction.

it means to be transformed by the renewing of our minds. Paul is more interested in helping us faithfully discern what it means not to be different from the world, but to be like Christ.

The ways of conformity

Our society tells us that our first priority should be to grow up by settling down and fitting in. In the late 1950s, a young person in France was supposed to grow up and be a patriotic Frenchman and, if necessary, to participate in efforts to violently suppress the Algerian rebellion. A young person growing up in Algeria during that time and for the same reason was supposed to come out on the opposite side of that war. In a religious and culturally conservative rural community, you should grow up to fit in there. This means defending that community's values, prejudices, and commitments against all kinds of outside threats. For those who grow up in mainstream North American society, "fitting in" means living up to North America's vision of life. This means installing high-fidelity audio and video in every room, cooking on a barbecue pit in the backyard, and faithfully attending "the church of your choice." As different as these patterns are, they share the fundamental assumption that to grow up is to fit in wherever you find yourself.

The most popular alternative to trying to fit in is to try to be different. Let us seek to affirm what the surrounding society denies and to deny what it affirms. Let us be different as a matter of principle. Every society, every church or college, has some people trying to do this. Some deviate to the right and some to the left of what they consider to be the middle. Some try to be different by being "higher" and others by being "lower" on the scale of the priorities of that society. What these rebels often do not see is that their rebellion is usually just as much a kind of conformity as that of blatant conformists. In fact, it is doubly so. The rebel is first a prisoner of the system that he or she rejects. Every time it says "yes," the rebel must say "no." Every time it says "no," the rebel must say "yes." Where it says "don't," rebels must do. Where it says "do," rebels don't. The rebel is also a prisoner of whatever group of rebels he or she has chosen to follow.

There is nothing more compulsive, not to mention boring, than the nonconformity of any one generation's set of rebels.

A choice of slaveries: wealth, war, and self

In light of these options, the apostle Paul is simply being realistic when he tells us that we have before us not a choice between freedom and slavery but only a choice of slaveries:

> When you were slaves of sin, you were free in regard to righteousness. So what advantage did you then get from the things of which you are now ashamed? The end of those things is death. But now that you have been freed from sin and enslaved to God, the advantage you get is sanctification. The end is eternal life. For the wages of sin is death, but the free gift of God is eternal life in Christ Jesus our Lord. (Romans 6:20-23)

Let us not be misled by the word *sin*. We have brushed this word aside in such a way that it seems only to apply to the distasteful, unworthy, corrupt, sensual, or crude. We tend to assume that adultery is sin in a sense that gossip is not. We regard murder or alcoholism as sin, but not greed. Nor do we consider patriotism, dilettantism, or ambition to be sinful. When the word *sin* has been redefined to apply only to the indecent, it is obvious that not every cause to which a person commits is "sin." But Paul is right in telling us that everything to which a person commits is a slavery.

Slavery is the oldest and most descriptive word for a value system—a pattern of responding to the world around us, a pattern to which we commit and which determines how we behave. Until recently, the phrase *to be committed* was used most often to refer to one's being placed in prison or under psychiatric care. Commitment is the loss of one's self-determination—the loss of control over all of one's activities.

The most popular slavery today is devotion to Mammon, the god of wealth. When we want to argue that time is important, we say, "time is money." When we want to convince others that education is desirable, we explain that if they go to college their total earnings will be hundreds of thousands more over the course of their career. People who argue that democracy is better than other systems of government are convincing only to the extent that they prove that free enterprise is more productive. In our society, all values are reduced to how much they pay or how they "work."

In the time of Jesus, this reduction of values to monetary standards was not as far-reaching. Job choices were not all made on the basis of income, and society's estimation of who is important was not made primarily on the basis of wealth. Even so, Jesus had to deal with people for whom the service of Mammon was truly a slavery. Such people could be freed for faith and discipleship only by being freed from their money. Let us not assume that students or others with little money are exempt from this temptation. The choices they make about gaining an education, spending their spare time, or waking up on Sunday mornings all reflect a commitment to one slavery or another. They all involve a choice about Mammon.

A close competitor of Mammon is Mars, the god of war. In reality, however, the two do not really compete. For instance, over half the American federal budget is devoted to preparation for aggressive military activity. It matters little whether we say here that Mars is helping Mammon or Mammon is helping Mars. In any case, militarism has nothing to do with the protective and orderly functions of the cop on the corner. People attempt to tell us that government, including war, is a kind of rational self-defense by which a society protects its tranquility and order against outside menaces through intelligent and appropriate means. Such an understanding will never grasp the reality of service to Mars. Militarism is a religious, nonrational commitment to self-glorification and to the assumption that things will never go right in God's world unless I am at once prosecutor, judge, jury, and hangman in the other person's case. What is wrong with militarism is not that, if ultimately war is declared, some people will be killed. What is most wrong with militarism is the idolatry of thinking that I or we or our government alone shall determine what things are worth killing others for.

But perhaps, you will say, my examples are inappropriate. Mars and Mammon are not immediately the gods of any educational or Christian institution. Does not the choice of such extreme and unwholesome kinds of slavery leave open the question of whether slavery can be avoided? Do we not have a vision of being able to rise above such crude choices?

Can we not be objective and open minded? Can we not suspend judgment, weigh one commitment against another, and limit our involvement?

This vision, I submit, is the greatest idol of all. For above and beneath, before and behind Mammon and Mars, the greatest idol is "me." To think that I am rising above the claims of society upon me—that I am deciding, and sometimes even deciding to make no decisions—is one of the most deeply entrenched ways to serve something other than God. To make no decisions, to keep one's mind completely open, to maintain a "balanced" and noncommittal attitude, is no less binding than any other way to live. It will inevitably take you down one rather than another of the tracks you might possibly choose. Years later, you will see that your decisions, investments, and energy were just as clearly committed to yourself and your independence as others have committed to causes outside themselves.

Slavery to righteousness

What the apostle Paul offers as an alternative is not liberation—seen negatively as freedom from a particular kind of bondage. He claims that there is no such thing. What he offers instead, as a gift of God's grace, is a new kind and a new degree of bondage. It is a new kind of bondage because it is the slavery for which we are made. It is a new degree of bondage because only this kind of commitment, which Paul calls "slavery to righteousness," can apply to every dimension of your life.

You can commit yourself religiously to open-mindedness or to opium, to automobile racing or to pacifism, to the American way of life or to your family. Each of these commitments can be made total, as far as you are humanly able. Yet each of these commitments will fail to address certain dimensions of your life, to meet certain needs, or to help with certain decisions. A passion for auto racing will not tell you how to retire. A passion for the English language's purity will not tell you when to marry. "Slavery to righteousness" is an alternative that belongs in a different category. Slavery to righteousness (or justice) is true freedom precisely because no part of my life needs to be distorted when I commit myself totally to what God wants me to be.

2

To Thine Own Self Be True?

It might not be exaggerating to claim that the most significant event in world history since the work of Jesus was the fourteenth- to fifteenth-century birth of the human. Those familiar with world literature and the history of civilization are aware of the sweeping change in mentalities that came from Renaissance humanism. This change brought about the idea that there *is* such a thing as the human—the human self and human nature—and that the highest goal of any individual's endeavor is self-realization.

Self-realization sickness and Jesus' healing word

North American civilization, in particular, has been built upon the foundation of self-realization. We have it in our political history with the concept of innate rights. We have it in our psychological history with the vision of the pioneer personality, the self-made person. The idea is always that the human has, or rather is, a "self" and that an individual's highest goal is the realization of what he or she can be.

No civilization has been more successful than ours in implementing this vision by creating institutions and expressions for it. Yet if we are to measure ourselves and our civilization by the statistical indexes of social health—juvenile crime, broken families, and mental illnesses—no civilization is sicker than ours. Sicker of what? We are sick of ourselves. That is the meaning of mental and social illness.

It is therefore a redeeming, saving, and liberating word that Jesus speaks, and not a crushing word of condemnation, when he says to his disciples, "Do not think that I have come to bring peace to the earth; I have not come to bring peace, but a sword. . . . Whoever loves father or mother more than me is not worthy of me; and whoever loves son or daughter more than me is not worthy of me; and whoever does not take up his cross and follow me is not worthy of me. Those who find their life will lose it, and those who lose their life for my sake will find it" (Matthew 10:34, 37-39). What Jesus rejects here is not selfishness in the crude animal sense alone. He also speaks to the nobler kind of self-esteem that stands at the heart of our civilization's best intentions. He critiques not only concern for one's own self, but also for the extended self, which is one's family. We are told we must hate not only self but mother and father, son and daughter (Luke 14:26).

Smuggling self-love back into Christianity

The great concern of Christian thought since the Renaissance has been to smuggle back into Christian thought the Stoic idea of being yourself, esteeming yourself, or realizing yourself. This is being done by those who argue that when Jesus says, "love your neighbor as yourself," he must mean first of all "love yourself." On the contrary, what he really means is, "you know full well what it means to love somebody because you do love yourself. Well, that is the way to love your neighbor."

Self-love is also smuggled back in through discussions of Christian self-sacrifice as a kind of inverted hedonism. Its proponents claim that giving up comforts and sensual pleasures in this life is worth it because it is eternally rewarded in the next life. Seventeenth-century French philosopher Blaise Pascal expresses this idea with his famous gamble, known as Pascal's wager. He reasoned with a kind of calculating selfishness that to believe in the existence of a divine order is worth the investment because acceptance of this order may pay out in the end. This sort of understanding has been favored by evangelists pleading with us to save at least our own soul. Yet the greatest people in the Bible—Paul of the New Testament and Moses of the Old—were actually willing to see themselves as religiously lost, cursed, and rejected by God if that meant God's purposes would go on.

The apostle Paul's idea of self

Paul went very far in his rejection of concern for himself. This showed in his preaching and in the way he worked. When Paul was ministering with and trying to win Jews, he kept all the rules of Jewish piety and purity (1 Corinthians 9:20). This inconvenienced him greatly and ultimately led to his arrest and imprisonment. When dealing with recent converts from paganism—who were eager to shake off all traces of pagan relationships and therefore were afraid to participate in idolatrous feasts by eating their meat—Paul said, "Then I'll be a vegetarian for life" (1 Corinthians 8:13, paraphrased). When relating to people who had no law at all, that is, with outright pagans, Paul made no issue of his principles. He was to them as someone without the law (1 Corinthians 9:21).

This kind of flexibility—patterning his own behavior so extensively after the tastes, behavior, and the culture of the people he was trying to win—ultimately leads to disintegration of personality. Paul had no home of his own. He had no cultural base where he could sit down, be himself, have his own standards, and live up to his own principles. He was always adapting to somebody. It is not at all difficult to understand why he was accused of trying to please people, of trying to please men in particular, of "commending himself" to others by his apparently unprincipled flexibility. Any psychological counselor can tell us how hard it is on people to have no base of their own, no home, no place where they belong and can take at least some things for granted. It is no wonder Paul could not have a wife along.

Mental health and the gospel

I just spoke of psychological health. We have learned in recent years that self-disparagement or neglecting one's own needs is unhealthy. It is a sign that something is wrong. It may indicate that people have learned to hate themselves. The path to mental health, and to effectiveness and usefulness for such people, is what the counselor calls self-acceptance. Is this one more effort to smuggle self-esteem back into Christian thought? It need not be.

It provides, however, a good chance to clarify one thing that Jesus did not mean. He did not mean that because we are not ultimately concerned with self we should no longer think about ourselves. It does not mean that we're unaware of our personality, our emotions, and our needs. He meant simply that these needs have no ultimate hold upon us compared to the call of the gospel. The apostle Paul, or even the prophet Jeremiah, provides clear proof that godly people can still be very bothered about their reactions, emotions, and feelings about where they belong. That's not what is wrong. What's wrong is making our self-esteem the standard of our decisions and behavior.

The second lesson that this insight from mental health tells us is that the only ground for forgetfulness of the self is awareness of God's kingdom and God's purpose in the world. We cannot make a virtue of self-abnegation in and of itself, as if anyone who forgets the self is doing a good thing. This is what some people take a selfish pride in doing. The self-forgetfulness of Paul, Moses, Jeremiah, and Jesus was possible only because they were keenly aware of what God was doing in the world. It was because of God's purposes that Jesus could forget to calculate his own interests, concerns, and needs.

Losing ourselves in God's purposes

What is it then that replaces the concept of the self and the concern for the self, if not that we simply turn our self-esteem inside out and make ourselves suffer? What is the standard? The standard is not a better philosophical absolute, as if instead of self-realization we should focus on realizing something else. The other standard is the reality of God's working in the world. It is what Jesus called his kingdom—finding embodiment and marching down through history in the form of people who are not the same as the world around them because of their commitment to what God has done in Jesus Christ.

What is really and most fundamentally wrong with self-realization is not that I see worth in myself, but that I make the decision about what is worthwhile in myself. It is not the concept of self-realization as a philosophical goal, but self-centeredness in making decisions about how I reach my goal that really matters. Overcoming the self as a value is only possible if we overcome the autonomy of the self as a way of making decisions. My commitment to the kingdom of God will only make a difference if it makes me bump into other people who see differently what I should be doing. Sacrifice of the self is only real if someone can stop me from my self-centered efforts to make my own decisions about whom to be, what to be, and how to be myself.

My commitment to a kingdom that is above myself and that replaces self-realization as a standard in my life can only be effective if there is something like what the New Testament calls "communion." It requires a group of people committed to the purposes beyond myself to which God has committed me. This is what we call the church—not the church as a denomination, as management framework, or as certain defined ministries—but the church as people.

What the church through which God is working asks of me and offers me is not conformity in a sense that would raise afresh the question, "Shall I be myself or not? Shall I deny myself or not?" It is instead a community of concern for God's purposes, which lie beyond all of ourselves in this world. It is only in losing our lives, losing ourselves in God's purposes, that we might again find ourselves for who we truly are. Every kind of worldly commitment creates among its disciples a deceptive sort of "communion." Yet the fellowship of those who bear one another's burdens, who restore one another in a spirit of meekness, who learn to accept one another despite their faults, is the only way truly to place something other than self-realization at the center of my purposes.

I can have a theory of God's overarching purposes, but as long as I decide from day to day what to do next, those purposes are just another way that my *self* comes back to the surface. I can get along without any theology, or with a pretty poor theology, if I find myself in the midst of a fellowship of persons concerned for one another and for God's redemptive work in the world. In this sort of fellowship we find a new definition of what it means to be conformed to Christ as his slaves.

This is the point of orientation for our nonconformity in this age. It is not a different set of principles, old or new. It is not an attempt to look at what the world is doing and just do it differently. It is not to see what the world used to be doing and do it again. Rather, it is finding ourselves called by God into a new kind of fellowship with a new kind of people, whose involvement in God's work in the world is such that the old ways of posing the question just don't fit anymore.

3

As If Not

We have already been reminded how self-evident it is for our society that to become an "adult" means to settle down and fit into a frame. The process of socializing, which includes education, is intended to aid the individual in this process. We have been told that our usefulness and happiness will depend upon how well and how rapidly we mature in this way. After all, the world needs reliable and steady citizens.

In fact we could say that who we are is where we fit in. A person's very identity is tied up in the place that he or she occupies in the social order. When people move about frequently from one job to another, we often say, "Those people have not yet found themselves."

Contemporary society's mobility and stability

Any society will promise security from the cradle to the grave to those who can be counted on to fit in. In the former Soviet Union, the system through which this happened was called socialism and was administered by a commissar. In North America, the system is called free enterprise and is administered by insurance agents, bankers, and pension plan administrators. In either case, the effect is basically the same. If you fit in you'll be all right. The expectation of security, thanks to the planning of someone else, is so universal that employers report that the crucial consideration of college seniors contemplating their first job is often, "What kind of pension plan do they have?"

We are quite aware that our society enables, and in fact needs, a great measure of geographical mobility. We can move more frequently and more freely from place to place than has ever been the case before. This is but a further demonstration of the extent to which people have become interchangeable. Your company can count on being able to move you from here to there because the function that you fill is that of a cogwheel in a machine, and cogwheels are interchangeable. The mobility of American society is made possible by its stability. Employers know exactly what each job category means and that anyone fitting that label can be counted on to fulfill that function.

Mennonites especially have always been stable people (no pun intended). We have been known for our solid communities in which for years—even hundreds of years—a church in a rural society can go on without adding any new names to the roster. So if at this point our church and our world agree, what questions could we possibly raise about whether it is right? Here I could develop my question gradually, attempting to unfold it Socratically. But for reasons of brevity, permit me to jump in at the other end of the discussion to demonstrate why this glorification of stability must be challenged from the perspective of the gospel.

The gospel's irresponsibility

The apostle Paul wrote to a very young church in the chaotic city of Corinth. If ever maturity and solidity were needed, if ever social stability were a task of the Christian church, Corinth was certainly the place. This was the place to concentrate on having reliable Christian business people and steady Christian families who bring up their children with the help of Christian schools. In this context, what does Paul say about social stability? He discusses marriage in particular, but he sees it in a far broader context. His advice is that people who are single should remain single and that widows should preferably not remarry. Those who marry do no wrong but it would be better not to do so.

> I mean, brothers and sisters, the appointed time has grown short; from now on, let even those who have wives be as though they had none, and those who mourn as though they were not mourning, and those who rejoice as though they were not rejoicing, and those who buy as though they had no possessions, and those who deal with the world as though they had no dealings with it. For the present form of this world is passing away. I want you to be free from anxieties. The unmarried man is anxious about the affairs of the Lord, how to please the Lord; but the married man is anxious about the affairs of the world, how to please his wife, and his interests are divided. . . . I say this for your own benefit, not to put any restraint upon you, but to promote good order and unhindered devotion to the Lord. (1 Corinthians 7:29-35)

It is no surprise that Paul has been psychoanalyzed for this passage. It has been taken to be a typical expression of a sour-grapes attitude of an old bachelor who just doesn't know any better. This explanation won't do. He was more likely a widower. Paul has also been theologically analyzed by people who say that his argument will only stand if you really believe the world is going to end within the next six weeks. This will not stand either. Paul's concern is for the differing significance of two realms: the realm of redemption and the realm of this world. This concern does not depend upon the length of time before the present pattern of things comes to an end.

Still there is no better word than *irresponsibility* to describe what Paul is here asking of the Christians of Corinth. He is saying that persons who have family obligations should live as if they had none. Men and women emotionally involved in their experience, who mourn or rejoice, should be as if this were not dominant in their life. Those who are involved in the economy, who buy and sell and deal with the world, should continue to do so but should act if it did not matter much. Do not let the normal obligations derived from your place in this society have an ultimate hold on you. This is Paul's point: "I would have you free to wait upon the Lord without distraction."

This was also the meaning of Jesus' concern for the rich young ruler whom he once told to sell all that he had. We misunderstand that instruction as well if we think Jesus was talking about stewardship, the desirability of helping the poor, or whether it is ethically possible and permissible to hold some or even much property. That was not the point. Jesus was telling that young man that if he was to be a disciple this would mean following Jesus—literally following him as he wandered around Palestine. You cannot do this if you are concerned with maintaining your equity. This young man was told to sell what he had because he was about to be remade as a disciple of the man who had no bed to call his own.

The aims of gospel mobility

This is the point at which Jesus' teaching to the rich young ruler, or Paul's instruction to the Christians in Corinth, speaks especially to young people today. Most of them may not be wealthy in terms of available cash, but all who attend college, by the virtue of their very presence in an educational institution and their accumulation of certain kinds of skills, are rich in mobility and rich in the capacity to make decisions. Most people in this world never get to make a free decision about where to live and what to do for a living. Only persons of considerable education have this extreme degree of liberty. It is this kind of liberty that the shiftlessness, the footlooseness of the gospel would have us take advantage of rather than seeking to settle in and find a place where society will dictate to us the norms of our obedience. Our concern should therefore be for *mobility*.

What does mobility look like practically? First of all, it means that we select our work with a view to real need. You can select your livelihood and your place of exercising it on the basis of security, as most college graduates are reported to do. You can make your choices with regard to the capacity to make a good living and to have a large backyard with a swimming pool. Or you can concentrate on those particular vocations that may be financially less rewarding and socially less stable and yet directly meet the needs of the neediest people. This will be one of the aims of our mobility.

Another aim should be *social creativity*. The chocolate manufacturers of Britain are businesses of Quaker origin. The chocolate manufacturers of the Netherlands are of

Mennonite origin. How did it happen that minority religious groups found themselves in this kind of business? It has a history. Sometime in the seventeenth or eighteenth centuries, when these minority religious groups were tolerated but not really legally accepted, all the normal positions of social leaderships in law and government, the university, the church, and medicine were reserved for the offspring of families within the official state church. The only place for others to use their industry and creativity was the brand new field of international commerce, which involved importing and processing goods from overseas.

It is no longer the case in our day that the field in which most creativity is needed is the importing and processing of chocolate. Yet we can find in this experience a model for how we might explore those realms in which creativity makes the most difference. Jesus said once that the dead should be left to bury the dead (Luke 9:60). This shows no disrespect for the dead. It shows an awareness that there are some functions in society that will be well taken care of without Christians investing their creativity in those functions. Someone else, in meeting such needs, can make a stable living. Burying the dead is still one of the businesses in which you can make a stable living. There are other such services that we can count on society handling by itself. Leadership in government and business are among these. Let us reserve our limited creativity for functions that will not be taken care of if we do not do it.

A further aim of our mobility should be our *identification with the disinherited*. The gods of all pagan faiths have been allied with the rich rulers. The priests of most religions are the employees of the landowners. But the God of Israel has always claimed to be with the poor—whether in the legislation of Deuteronomy, the words of the prophets, or the experiences of the New Testament. Our God is on the side of the poor. Our own choice of places to serve should be dictated by this divine preference. Let our choice also be dictated by the universality of our loyalties, not to one nation or class but to all people and to all classes. Let us seek the kind of occupations that will testify to our broad concern for all people and to the limited nature of our loyalty to any one nation, class, or culture.

On managing the liberty we have

Now, permit me to make two daring and unpopular proposals. Might we be so honest as to give some attention to what Paul says directly on the subject of the passage we read? Can we admit that remaining single for another year or two increases our usefulness for some kinds of service? Can nothing be done about the contemporary American drive to marry younger? There is nothing wrong with marriage. But what is so right about being in this much haste? Compared to the other needs in this world, what reasons do we have to be hasty?

Lastly, we might also consider some of the traditional concerns that have fallen under the heading of nonconformity, for instance, the way we use our leisure time, our choice of vocabulary, and our choice of cultural patterns. If we should think as our Mennonite ancestors did that the reason for these patterns is that they are in the Bible or that if we do not make such choices we shall stand condemned, this would be wrong. But we are no longer in danger of this error. Might it be that some of the patterns that Christians in their simplicity have found for expressing their faithfulness might still give us guidance—not about how to be right and perfect and worthy of merit—but how to be good stewards of our time and our creativity?

In a magazine my children read, there was the question, "Say what is wrong with this statement: Billy was going to a contest to see who could eat the most watermelon, so before he went he practiced by eating as much as he could at home." There was nothing wrong with eating watermelon at home, but if Billy had been a steward of his capacity to do later what he wanted to do, he wouldn't have practiced in this way.

Let us get over the lazy habit of assuming that every decision in the Christian life is a matter of whether a deed is absolutely wrong or absolutely obligatory. Instead, let us realize that there are realms in which our responsibility is the best possible management of the liberty we have. Let us attempt to see, with a new degree of respect and cultural imagination, the sum total of the decisions of some of our ancestors as incorporating the kinds of insight that may even have suggestions for today.

4

Godly Arrogance

One of the most precious achievements of education is modesty. By this I mean a capacity for self-criticism and a capacity to overcome our provincialism. Provincialism is a childish kind of arrogance, the childishness of having closed oneself off from other alternatives. The fruit of provincialism is the thought that one's own world is the only world—that the way we see things is the way they truly are. This we need to criticize, not only to overcome our own narrowness, but to gain a deepened concern for the needs and convictions of others and to avoid unintended offense and imbalance.

We have thus learned—and we needed to learn—to cut ourselves down to size. We needed to look at our own convictions, theories, and practices in the light of a deepened awareness that there are other ways of seeing and doing things. Some of the ideas and practices that we have rethought and become modest about have been objects of sincere and profound religious devotion. For this reason, we must be careful when cutting ourselves down to size that we do not also cut God down to our size.

We have become so accustomed to testing, explaining, and sometimes apologizing for our cultural quirks and peculiar convictions that, even more than the world around us, we may think that we must apologize for our God. Among unfamiliar company it can happen that we only acknowledge our Christian commitment when we are pushed into it. It isn't something that overflows. It isn't something we always think our neighbor needs. When we are called upon to explain why it is that we think this or that, we say that it's somehow the fault of our parents or "because my grandfather was an Amishman."

Recovering the New Testament's missionary arrogance

I do not intend to challenge the need for growth in modesty and in cultural perspective, but I do intend to challenge the tendency to make a hobby out of a corrective. Today's most urgent need is no longer perspective and modesty. What today's world and church need most is a recovery of the missionary arrogance of the New Testament church. *To arrogate* (the verb from which we get the unpopular adjective *arrogant*) means to make claims for oneself or for one's cause. If the claims we make are for ourselves, then it is understandable why we need to overcome our arrogance. But if the cause for which we are making claims is the cause of the one true God, then anything short of absolute demands is unfaithfulness.

At this point the New Testament church was unwavering. It is not easy to select a sermon or a letter from the New Testament that would especially symbolize or typify the astounding claims that the New Testament church was making. Its confidence was so pervasive that it never needed to be pointed out.

Take, for example, the apostle Paul's speech that he made to the least sympathetic body of listeners he is reported to have spoken to: a group of philosophers in Athens. He began with a statement that these philosophers could very well understand in their own terms, but then closed with the following bold claim:

> Since we are God's offspring, we ought not to think that the deity is like gold, or silver, or stone, an image formed by the art and imagination of mortals. While God has overlooked the times of human ignorance, now he commands all people everywhere to repent, because he has fixed a day on which he will have the world judged in righteousness by a man whom he has

appointed, and of this he has given assurance to all by
raising him from the dead. (Acts 17:29-31)

This was preposterous to the philosophers. The idea that
some man, not an idea, truth, or concept, but a man of
whom they had not even heard—an unphilosophical man,
a Jew who was already dead—was going to judge the world
was simply absurd to the philosophers. Worse yet, Paul
maintained that this claim was certified by the resurrection.
This last point could not have meant much to the Greeks.
They did not care very much about the body. Did Paul not
know any better? Could he find no better way of making his
point less crudely?

That is just Paul's point. When we preach the Christian
gospel we are not talking about ideas but reporting events. We
are not talking only about past events that can be studied by
historians, but future events about which only our faith makes
us sure. These events have not happened yet, and it is only the
certainty of future events that has kept the Christian church
alive and will keep us alive over the centuries. When I speak of
certainty I do not mean the subjective certainty of feeling reas-
sured, but the objective certainty of what is sure to happen.

Let us attempt to illustrate by remembering the difference
between a taxi cab and a train. The taxi driver will only make a
trip if you are interested in making it at your expense. He lives
from your desire to make such trips. The trip is made when you
want to make it and by the itinerary you choose. Should you
get another taxi, that one will also take you where you want
to go. It is not that way with trains. The train has a schedule
that was fixed long before you became interested in your trip.
If you get on the wrong train you end up at the wrong place. If
you are not on board when the train leaves, you won't get to
your destination at all.

Too often the pleas of evangelists or of parents and teach-
ers who are trying to move us to make faith decisions have
risked giving us the impression that the kingdom of God is
like a taxi. They lead us to believe that whether it ever really
happens will depend upon whether we want to go there.
Nothing could be more false. It is perhaps not accidental
that the well-known spirituals speak of the gospel not as an
automobile but as a train. If you don't "get on board" it is

leaving just the same. If you prefer to go somewhere else, it is going nonetheless to its heavenly terminal.

The coming of the kingdom of God is unstoppable. We need to be reminded that God's reign is not a democracy. It doesn't depend on the consent of the governed. God's kingdom and the certainty of the ultimate triumph of God's purposes in, for, and beyond history is a fact. You don't vote on facts. A fact just is. You believe it and adjust to it, or you are damned.

A mark of the problematic character of our "modesty" and "perspective" is the way we have let strong language be the trademark of people who have nothing strong to say. We have confused the gentility of weak conviction with the gentleness of witnessing.

God's overpowering reality and nonconformity

How would Christians be different if they truly believed that God is an overpowering reality as revealed in the work of the Son? We would probably stop trying to measure our commitment by other people's standards. This is the root of nonconformity. We would not make our day-to-day ethical decisions about minor matters on the basis of whether anybody is watching. We would not make our decisions about the use of violence and power to accomplish our purposes by calculating what is possible and what the results are likely to be. When the resurrection is the center of our message, human standards of possibility do not apply. When all the doors are closed, God opens a window or takes off the roof.

We would not measure our attitudes toward the American way of life by whether they are acceptable to our neighbors. We would not measure our commitment to the vision of a believers church, a committed fellowship of people responsible for one another, by whether all Christians everywhere happen to be looking for just this.

We would not let our standards be determined by Immanuel Kant's famous question, "Could everybody do it?" This is, of course, how most Westerners think about ethics. I can't ask of myself, I can't even ask of fellow Christians, any specific action unless I believe I can prove that society would work well if everyone else did the same. This is a hard standard to meet with some ethical questions. It is also a standard that the Christian should not try to meet, for there is no likelihood that everyone will decide and behave as if God were the ultimate reality. Yet Christians alone have accepted God's call to decide and behave in light of this reality.

The particular temptation of contemporary Christian communities is to tailor our beliefs so that they are socially respectable. Whether our beliefs are respectable or not varies from place to place and time to time. Right now it happens that in Western society there is a growing awareness of the relevance of Christian commitment. But if this were not the case, it should be no less surely and no less arrogantly our commitment. We must not let our decisions about Christian obedience be measured by what our neighbors would consider "socially responsible."

We can make a pretty good case for the social fruitfulness of nonconformity. It can even be argued that society's survival depends more upon the people who are different than upon those who are the same. This could be demonstrated at great length by people who study the history of society. It can even be claimed that Christians who are not slavishly committed to the survival of their nation can contribute spiritually—and in the long run most effectively—to the moral survival of their nation's values. Yet even if that were not the case or if we could not prove it, our Christian commitment to the obedience of suffering discipleship should be no different.

Let us therefore face squarely the temptation to think that gaining perspective is a matter of learning to think in terms of the other person's values or those of the wider society. Let us resist the misplaced hope that we can still reserve somewhere a small cranny for the valid remainders of the commitment of faith from which we came. This would be making faith a footnote or an appendage to a body of knowledge that we got somewhere else and a set of values that we adopted because that is how society works.

Let us have the nerve, the conviction—perhaps even the *arrogance*—to claim, in spite of all our modesty and awareness of our inability to represent God perfectly, that the only ultimate values and realities are those that have been revealed in this one man Jesus—who will judge the world and will judge it justly because he has risen from the dead.

5

Divine Foolishness

Three Anabaptists were discussing baptism with three pastors of the Swiss state church in August 1525, when a fourth Anabaptist entered the house. He knew nothing about what they had just been discussing. What he said, therefore, all the more faithfully illustrates the general tone of the movement he represented. He broke into the discussion with the outburst, "What we need is divine wisdom: to perceive honor in the cross, and life in death—to deny yourselves and become fools."[1]

On being gospel misfits

Behind all differences in behavior between Christians and others (and for that matter behind all similarities in behavior) lies a commitment to God's identity and purposes in the world through Jesus Christ that makes us misfits. We are misfits not because we represent another culture or another world. We have noted to what extreme lengths the apostle

---

1. Here Yoder is referring to Lorenz Hochrütiner's statement, "We are in need of divine wisdom, in which honour is found in the cross, and life is found in death, and we must look like and become fools." See John Howard Yoder, *Anabaptism and Reformation in Switzerland* (Kitchener, ON: Pandora Press, 2004), 292.

Paul went in adapting to the scruples of recent converts, to the legalism of certain Jews, or to the unprincipled liberty of the pagans. But we are misfits because of a commitment— and anyone who is familiar with correctional facilities or psychiatric hospitals knows that commitment means a loss of self-determination—to a man who was crucified because he troubled Jewish piety and Roman politics.

That man's cross is the symbol of the eternal conflict that arises when the divine invasion of history through the man "with whom [God is] well pleased" (Matthew 3:17) intersects with the powers of creaturely rebellion and when rebellion, for the time being, has the last word. That is the cross. The apostle Paul spoke not only of what we technically call "atonement" or the "forgiveness of sins." He spoke about the whole pattern of God's work in the world when he wrote to the Christians at Corinth:

> For the message about the cross is foolishness to those who are perishing, but to us who are being saved it is the power of God. For it is written, "I will destroy the wisdom of the wise, and the discernment of the discerning I will thwart." Where is the one who is wise? Where is the scribe? Where is the debater of this age? Has not God made foolish the wisdom of the world? For since, in the wisdom of God, the world did not know God through wisdom, God decided, through the foolishness of our proclamation, to save those who believe. For Jews demand signs and Greeks desire wisdom, but we proclaim Christ crucified, a stumbling block to Jews and foolishness to Gentiles, but to those who are the called, both Jews and Greeks, Christ the power of God and the wisdom of God. (1 Corinthians 1:18-24)

Recent Bible studies have clarified the difference between Greek and Hebraic mentalities. But what Paul says here is that God confounds both equally. We can best understand the scandal of our nonconformity today by seeing in these two mentalities the two structures of respectability against which, even today, the Christian accepts being foolish.

The Greek was looking for valid generalities. When Paul began his speech at Athens, he began with valid generalities. He said that God had created the world, had made all people of one blood, had given each nation a place to dwell, and that God was spirit and was not really contained by temples and images. They could understand all of these statements because they were all valid generalities. But then Paul said that a day is coming—a day when God will judge the world through a man, *one* man, who was resurrected. That was the end of the discussion in Athens.

Nonconformity and the scandal of particularity

We are face to face with "the scandal of the particular." The profound German philosopher, Gotthold Lessing, stated this in a classic way, saying, "What I am looking for is a universal truth of reason, and what you have to give is an accidental truth of history."[2] Even if the "accidental" truth is true, it doesn't prove anything generally valid. This is correct.

The apostle is here proclaiming as the wisdom of God that what matters the most for all history happened to the body of one particular Galilean woodworker on one particular hillside in occupied Judea on one particular Friday about a hundred thousand Fridays ago. If we were a church according to the New Testament, it is not sure we would celebrate Easter once a year. Easter is every Sunday. We probably would not celebrate an annual Christmas either. But there is one peg in history, one Friday, irrevocably fixed at one time in Passover Week, and one place outside the walls of which is the very center, according to Paul, of the wisdom he preached.

We must still accept the scandal of the particular if Christian conformity to Christ is to be visible—as it must be. If our conformity to Christ is to be united—and it must be—Christians in every time and place must, through a completely human process of thought, settle on what it means to respond there to the challenge of their day. This means making a particular decision of crucial importance where another particular decision would have also been logically possible.

---

2. See Gotthold Ephraim Lessing, *Lessing's Theological Writings*, trans. Henry Chadwick (Stanford, CA: Stanford University Press, 1957), 53: "Accidental truths of history can never become the proof of necessary truths of reason."

It was decided once in the sixteenth century by some of God's people that the issue of infant baptism was the place where they were called to focus their nonconformity in order to challenge worldly views of what it means to be Christian. In other centuries, other groups of God's people decided what patterns of dress were called for in order to challenge worldly displays of wealth or of the body. In still other times and places, Christians have concentrated upon certain patterns of conscientious objection to challenge this world's trust in the sword. In future times and places, Christians might be called to fix upon new ways of coming together for worship or new patterns of property ownership to challenge the particular idolatries of their century. During all such times and places, the pattern of nonconformed obedience will, if it is historically relevant at all, bear the traces of having been worked out in one time and one place to meet one challenge. For this reason, it will therefore not be universally valid. Obedience continues to be "folly to the Greeks."

Then the Jews must have been a people after God's own heart. They looked back to one man, Moses, to one law which was given to them on one mountain, and to one temple in Jerusalem. Yet somehow that was still not enough. Precisely because Jews were on God's wavelength with their particularities, it was all the more clear that there remained a conflict between their sense of God's particular working in history and what God really wanted to do. The Jews were looking for a "sign," for an effective work of God in history. They had known such signs in the past (think of the Red Sea) and they expected such signs in the future. Then this man Jesus came and claimed to be what they were waiting for. He talked about a "kingdom," he let himself be handled as a common criminal, and that was the end of him. And we're supposed to believe in that?

The scandal of the cross's ineffectiveness

The cross continues to be a stumbling block to many Jews. In parts of the world that have been influenced by the Judeo-Christian tradition (including the world of Islam), we believe that history is meaningful. We believe that it is "linear," that human experience is going somewhere and that it is has purpose. Here the scandal of the gospel is the ineffectiveness of the cross. If you work the way Jesus did, you won't get anything done.

This is why we have had to develop doctrines of the atonement that separate the death of Christ from what it meant to him morally, humanly, and historically to die as he did. We make of his death a kind of metaphysical transaction, either with the devil or with a vindictive God. One or the other demanded that there be a death, independently of what it actually meant for Jesus to die. In this way, theology has been trying to get away from the fact that the New Testament presents Jesus' death as the profoundest possible revelation of God. The very nature of God is suffering love, which leaves for later the triumph to which God is by nature entitled. So it remains today that "the way" to which we are called is the way of the cross. That way is not a theory about what God does in order to forgive, but what God did because God is forgiving.

We still face in our institutions and in our attitude toward politics, the family, survival, and economics the stumbling block of the ineffectiveness of it all. In the face of the Greek search for valid generalities, the cross is scandalous because it is particular, historical, and time-bound. Still deeper, in the face of the Western Hebraic tendency to glorify effectiveness and to envision the meaningfulness of human events, the way of the cross is a stumbling block.

We cannot say that if all American Christians were pacifists, Castro would shave off his beard or Khrushchev would keep on his shoes; all that we know is that God did not send bombers into that garden to free the Son from an unworthy fate. If we give all our goods to feed the poor, the gospel does not promise that there will no longer be hunger and social conflict. All we know for sure is that we serve a God whose very nature was to empty God's very self, becoming a slave even unto death. This God sealed the triumph of faithfulness to suffering love with the inexplicable, incalculable, impossible victory of the resurrection.

Part Two

Reshaping Nonconformity

6

The Subtle Worldliness[1]

Few things are so clearly assumed by the Bible than that Christians should be different. The type of argument one finds in the New Testament is not, "Since you should do x, therefore you will be different from the world." It is rather, "Since you are different from the world, therefore you should do x." The difference between Christians and the world is assumed, but it is not the goal of New Testament teaching.

Yet those of us who are most attached to the idea of nonconformity would be the most surprised to find that when the Bible speaks most strongly about Christian difference, it is not interested in matters that we habitually consider worldly. Biblical nonconformity is more concerned with issues that we routinely associate with good common sense and respectable citizenship.

Confusion of church and state

Already in the time of Christ, one of God's chief competitors for people's loyalty was Caesar, who was worshiped by the Roman state. Christians refused emperor worship as long as

---

1. "The Subtle Worldliness," *Gospel Herald* (December 21, 1954): 1209, 1221.

they were persecuted. But in the fourth century, when the church was tolerated under Constantine and then made the state religion under Theodosius, church leaders somehow lost their capacity for critical judgment and came to accept state patronage as normal and desirable. The resulting confusion of church and world has contaminated Christian thinking, action, and witness from their day to ours. One of the first forms of nonconformity must be found in this realm. We must regain the capacity to analyze and judge, in the light of Christian truth, the claims of state and society upon the Christian.

The present demoralized status of the Western world may be largely traced to an outgrowth of the church-world confusion connected with Constantine's epoch, but most clearly revealed in the Crusades. The crusader's philosophy may be summarized in three affirmations:

1. My country's social order is right, so it is willed by God.
2. My country's enemies are therefore wholly in the wrong.
3. Any means to force the submission of any enemy must therefore be pleasing to God.

These affirmations, though accepted by all of "Christian Europe" in the Middle Ages, are utterly pagan. The first denies that every social order is subject to God's judgment for its injustices. The second denies that all people are equal before God and treats as pure good or pure evil[2] what are really varying combinations of both. The third denies that love is the only right means to a good end.

All would be well and good if this medieval mentality had been denounced and abandoned by the Reformation and the Renaissance. Alas, such was not the case. This same mentality continued to justify wars of religion (where it was used on both sides), wars of imperialism, and wars of ideology, up to the present day. Not only is this mentality bad Christianity, since

---

2. Yoder's original wording here, and elsewhere in this essay, was "black" and "white" which, though acceptable in the era, is currently problematic in terms of racist connotations.

it blames God for human sin, it is even bad politics, since it denies the possibility of compromise and negotiation between varying shades of gray, which is the essence of real statesmanship. The real origin of wars is not in the politician's mentality, which would rather seek a tolerable compromise, but in the crusader's mentality, which claims that "God is on our side" and sets out, in terms of pure "evil" and pure "good," to defeat the powers of evil. Such powers have been identified with the Turks, the Albigenses, the Papists, the Protestants, George III, the southern slave owners, the Germans, the Japanese, and the Russians, to name only a few. Once the battle is won, the crusader is dismayed, or at least those who believed him and fought for him are dismayed, to discover in the "good" camp a new villain or in the defeated "evil" camp a new hero, and the crusade has to be done all over again.

Europe has now had enough. Nobody believes in crusades anymore. Since crusades were so closely associated with God and good, many don't believe in God or good anymore. Only two countries still believe in crusades, and that's why the world fears them both.[3] America, at least the America which Europe and Asia see, is planning busily for a crusade in the name of morality. Russia at least has the honesty to be cynical and to admit that her faith is materialism, which saves her the trouble of twisting Christian principles to fit her plans.

The most glaring inconsistency in the crusaders' position is the need, in order to bolster their own conviction, to deny both that their record is less than pure good (which excludes the Christian virtue of repentance) and that their adversary's position is better than pure evil (which excludes Christian charity). This obliges the crusaders to turn occasional somersaults that fool no one but themselves.

A while back the world was nearing the end of a crusade whose purpose was to disarm forever Germany and Japan ("evil") with the help of Russia ("good"). The men who

---

3. At the time Yoder wrote this article the Cold War was at its height. That era is now over. Yet what Yoder says is no less true today than it was in the 1950s. The never-ending war on terror, in which civilians are deliberately targeted both by extremist Muslims and the American military—through drone strikes and other military means—is a current example of Yoder's point.

gave their lives and their families were told that their cause was noble ("good") and that enemy soldiers were beasts. The same sort of crusade was later prepared again, but this time Russia was "evil" and Germans and Japanese were the best soldiers. The vice president of the United States went so far as to tell the Japanese, and at the same time the parents of those who fell in World War II, that the disarmament of Japan, for which that war was fought, was a mistake.

The more recent crisis of Indochina is a still more striking example. There was a time when America was the hope of oppressed peoples because of its devotion to freedom. Britain and the Netherlands had given up the Indies, but French colonialism, whose methods were more and more repressive and whose purposes were increasingly dictated by monetary interests, was whitewashed since it joined the battle against communism. American funds subsidized a war that without them might have ended long before. Communist China, being "evil" by definition, was iniquitous and guilty of aggression for providing material to the insurrectionist troops. America, being "good," was holding the free world together when it did the same for the French forces. The certainty of being on God's side, which was psychologically possible for Americans in the defense of America, stretches anyone's credulity too far when the police states of Spain, Yugoslavia, Formosa, and Morocco were claimed to be on God's side, too, since they shared opposition to Russia.

There was a time when aggressive war was condemned and each warring nation sought to label the other as the aggressor. Even this scruple has been washed away. The first threat to use the atom bomb came not from the cynical communists, but from American crusaders, who claimed to be putting morality back into politics.

Vigilant nonconformity to the crusading mentality

Where in relation to all this confusion is the place of the Christian? Nothing could be farther from the truth than to remain willfully ignorant of events in the social and political world. Our obligation is not limited to conscientious objection, relief work, and evangelism. Both the Old Testament prophets and Jesus clearly stated God's judgment on current events. Jesus' temple cleansing expressed judgment upon the economic order of his day. His teaching on Caesar, the temple tax, and the second mile, his demands on the rich young ruler, and his impact on Zacchaeus all rendered judgment upon social and political matters. Our nonconformity should not consist of ignorance or withdrawal, but the exercise of independent judgment and the continual application of basic Christian truths.

The first truth we must apply is that no cause is all "good." Every human enterprise stands under God's righteous judgment for falling short of both the love of Christ and the justice of the Ten Commandments. The second truth is that no enemy is all "evil." Every person bears traces of God's image and Christ died for all. Third, no good end can be served by evil means. One cannot gather figs from thistles, nor protect the innocent through mass destruction.

Our nonconformity therefore means never-ending vigilance. We must continually refuse to think in the good-and-evil patterns offered to us by the press and other means of mass communication. We must reject among our class or nation any crusading mentality. We must never give uncritical allegiance to any social, economic, or political system. Our uncritical allegiance is to the kingdom of God. That loyalty allows no taking sides in conflicts on another level and forbids giving even silent consent to any nation's absolute claims.

7

The Respectable Worldliness[1]

Christ's strongest teaching on worldliness is a passage from his Sermon on the Mount. It begins, "Do not store up for yourselves treasures on earth" (Matthew 6:19). That this is a matter of worldliness is clear in Jesus' warning in the middle of this passage that "no one can serve two masters" (v. 24) and in his concluding remark that pagans seek after such things while his followers seek first God's kingdom (v. 32).

Worldliness is not a specific action or set of actions that are wrong because they are forbidden. If that were the case, doing the right thing would simply be a matter of avoiding forbidden activities. Worldliness is not a special sort of depravity. It is the normal behavior of worldly people. It is any thought or behavior whose first concern is not God's kingdom and God's righteousness. And since worldly people can be quite respectable, there are also respectable forms of worldliness, some of which Jesus names in this passage.

Wealth and worldliness

It is worth noticing that many who accept a literal understanding of Matthew 5, John 13, and 1 Corinthians 11 have

---

1. "The Respectable Worldliness," *Christian Living* (January 1955): 14–15, 48.

little difficulty "interpreting" Jesus' warning against accumulating earthly wealth. It is simply a command for which the
Lord wants obedience. This passage belongs in the Sermon
on the Mount just as clearly as does "love your enemies" or
"swear not."

People who make accumulating wealth a major concern
in life are often not misers or lovers of extravagance. Often
they are sensible people making thoughtful arrangements for
old age or for their children. Yet it is precisely this sort of
forethought, and not a more extreme form of greed, that the
Lord seems to be criticizing when he tells us "do not worry
about your life . . . or about your body" (Matthew 6:25).

The question for Christ is one of confidence, or faith. He
does not advocate a happy-go-lucky existence whose motto
is "tomorrow will take care of itself." Christ reminds us that
God will take care of tomorrow, which is quite a different
matter. He does not ask lackadaisical or shortsighted disciples to think of the future. He asks for faith in the Father
whose love he describes as overflowing: "If you . . . know
how to give good gifts to your children, *how much more*
will the heavenly Father" (Luke 11:13). "If God so clothes
the grass of the field . . . will he not *much more* clothe you?"
(Matthew 6:30). Because "much more" is the only way to
speak of the Father's love, Christian faith means entrusting
oneself to God's care.

The opposite of faith in this passage is not unbelief. Jesus
tells us here that the opposite of faith is anxiety. Centuries
before psychologists began analyzing the "drives" and "complexes" of the human will, Jesus tells us that seeking after
wealth is a sign of anxiety, not industry or respectability. Not
knowing or daring to trust God, unbelievers seek substitutes
to reassure themselves. They think they have found one when
through shrewdness or hard work they accumulate sufficient
reserves to cover every eventual expense.

The first mistake such people make is pointed out at the
beginning of Jesus' teaching on the subject. "Moth and rust
consume . . . thieves break in and steal" (Matthew 6:19-20).
What thieves and moths did in Jesus' time, inflation, reces-
sion, and depression do in ours. The most evident error in
depending on wealth comes from the fact that wealth is not
dependable.

A deeper misjudgment is revealed by the parable in Luke's gospel where the Lord applies the word *fool* (a term so strong that in Matthew 5:22, Jesus tells us not to use it) to a successful farmer (Luke 12:13-21). The "rich fool" was foolish because his precautions, however adequate they may have seemed for the daily needs of food, drink, and merriment, did not deal with his deepest need. His deepest need was on another level: "This very night," God tells him, "your life is being demanded of you" (Luke 12:20). This sober announcement upset all his calculations. His many years of stockpiling goods had not truly calmed the anxiety he felt in his unbelief. It had only smothered it. When faced with life's most basic question—the question of death—he was unprepared.

Jesus probes still deeper. If a person will not serve God wholly and sacrificially, the alternative is not neutrality, half-time service, or even Sunday morning services. The one who does not serve God serves Mammon (Matthew 6:24). Jesus deems the accumulation of wealth as neither risky nor inadequate, though it is both. He condemns it most profoundly as idolatry. Either we serve God, laying up treasures in heaven and our "whole body will be full of light," or we worship Mammon, laying up perishable treasures and filling our body with darkness. A person must have a goal in life. Because it seeks security apart from God, wealth makes one of the strongest claims to replace God as that goal.

Wealth in Christian and world history

Saint Francis understood his discipleship as commitment to a life of poverty. The monastic tradition considers the abandonment of private property as a positive virtue. This is not necessarily the Lord's meaning here. Jesus adds to his warning the promise that "all these things will be given to you" (Matthew 6:33). What is asked of us is not principled poverty, but a willingness to share the poverty of our neighbor, which will sometimes mean practical poverty. He asks us not to abandon possession but to live "as if [we] had no possessions" (1 Corinthians 7:29-31), to live as free from our possessions as if we had none.

Mennonite history illustrates how spiritual life can suffer more from the sort of worldliness uncovered here than from any other cause. Insulated from baser forms of immorality by a stern ethical tradition and protected from violence, dishonesty, and political ambition by their tradition of nonresistance and truth-telling, Mennonites were often unprepared to meet the temptations of freedom and ease. When persecuted, they remembered well their need for faith. They lived and died in that faith. When tolerated and even favored, they prospered and sometimes forgot their need for confidence in God. They learned to become rich for themselves and not for God, just like the man in Jesus' parable. They were no longer obligated to discover the perilous faith that leans on God alone. Their industry and frugality rapidly earned them respect and security.

In the seventeenth century, a Dutch Mennonite minister recounted the fable of a demons' council. After persecution, violence, carnality, and revelry failed to entice the Anabaptists from the firmness of their devotion, it was decided to conquer them through wealth, the subtlest worldliness.[2] "For where your treasure is, there your heart will be also" (Matthew 6:21). This parable would apply equally to Christians from other traditions.

World history has seen plenty of wealthy people and wealthy nations. But never before has the world seen what it now witnesses in North America. Prosperity is considered the normal condition of a person. Elsewhere in the world there are telephones, central heating, and luxurious automobiles, but they belong to the wealthy minority. Here such comforts are considered normal and even necessary for decent living. Should anyone hesitate to believe this, the advertising industry is there to encourage covetousness by convincing us that every new luxury is a need. The worldliness of wealth and ease takes on a new degree of seriousness for North American Christians.

---

2. Yoder is referring to Galenus Abrahamsz, "De Doopsgezinden in de wereld," in *Geschiedenis der Doopsgezinden in Nederland*, ed. N. Van der Zijpp (Arnhem: Van Loghum Slaterus, 1952), 153–54. See also Cornelius J. Dyck, *Introduction to Mennonite History*, 3rd edition (Scottdale, PA.: Herald Press, 1993), 131; and Karl Koop, "Dangers of Superabundance: Pieter Pietersz, Mennonites, and Greed during the Dutch Golden Age," *Journal of Mennonite Studies* 27(2009): 63.

Use of our means

Why has such wealth become so common? Some credit belongs to hard-working people. With a strong sense of equality and fair play, they have made the most of their opportunities for the common good. Other factors have nothing to do with credit or blame. For example, rich natural resources and the psychological stimulation of frontier conditions have played an important role. Yet other reasons require serious criticism. Consider the wasteful exploitation of natural resources, wars fought on foreign soil, unequal treatment of immigrant and migrant labor, tariff barriers, and price supports that prevent other nations from trading freely with us. All of this has contributed to an unheard-of standard of living.

As much as some of our wealth is honestly won, let us also recognize the hand of God, who not only laid in the earth its treasures but also provided the industry and honesty of the early settlers. We must be careful that the secularizing power of wealth does not destroy its roots, as has been the case in other ages and cultures. Where that wealth has been won otherwise than through useful labor, let us recognize and dare to point out that humanity's sin stands before God's judgment. We cannot avoid involvement in the false prosperity of war or protectionism, but we can and should witness against the sin that brought it about and refuse to keep the wealth that war, tariff, and luxury bring.

What matters most is the use we make of our means. The Pharisees in Jesus' time, and many believers in our day, felt that this duty was done with the tithe. Yet Jesus' only mention of the tithe was unfavorable. He did not object that it is too much to ask, but that it is ten times too little. It hides the real problem of stewardship, which is that every cent belongs to God and must be used to God's glory.

Jesus begins by warning us against accumulating wealth for ourselves, since God will take care of tomorrow. What then of old age, sickness, or loss of the breadwinner? The Bible's answer is that pure religion means caring for widows and orphans (James 1:27) and that serving the sick and needy is serving Christ (Matthew 25:31-46). Both the question of saving and that of life insurance are falsely stated when the choice is between making careful arrangements for the future and making none.

God offers a third option. Families should care for the aged, and churches should care for the family-less and abandoned (1 Timothy 5:4-16). The alternative to commercial endowment and life insurance is not a rule against them, but the kind of Christian giving for which they are a secular substitute. The fact that confidence in commercial insurance has become prevalent is a sign that the church has not responded to her obligation to care for the needy *as one cares for oneself*. It would be difficult to prove that in the majority of cases widows are so well provided for by the Christian fellowship that the church has a moral right to forbid the use of commercial insurance.

A recent note in *Christian Living* magazine asked what we would be doing for Christ if our fat barns, automobiles, and general prosperity were suddenly dissolved. That is an interesting hypothetical question. But the question that we should be more concerned about is not hypothetical. What are we doing for Christ *with* our general prosperity and all the means it puts in our hands? When our relief and mission agencies are unable to enter all the doors for service and witness that open to them, largely for financial reasons, it seems clear that the answer is not that we are doing enough!

It is a pleasant form of recreation and food for self-righteousness to meditate on other people's sins. Thinking about how much other people spend for cosmetics, alcohol, tobacco, and amusements creates a happy feeling in the breast of those who spend just as much for unnecessarily new automobiles, household appliances, vacationing, and bank accounts. Before the judgment of Christ, the fact that one sort of worldliness is more respectable than another seems to make little difference.

We can never remind ourselves often enough that sin for the Christian disciple is not a matter of doing what is forbidden. Sin is doing anything less than the very best one knows. Nowhere in the Bible is the use of alcohol, the purchase of two-hundred-horsepower automobiles, the construction of larger church buildings, attendance at movie theaters, airplane travel, or the eating of meat offered to idols expressly forbidden. In each case the question must be answered in a concrete situation, with the guidance of the Spirit, and on the basis of one question: If our purpose in life is to offer ourselves as a living sacrifice to God and to fellow human beings, what is the best possible use of our time, talents, and wealth? It will be the case that, in order for our living sacrifice to be the most effective, we will sometimes be called, not by prudence but by conviction, to invest in our own health, in equipment for living or for producing, in education, or in recreation. Again, the Christian life is not a matter of rules that are definable once and for all for everyone. It is a matter of constantly living under the leading of God. The Bible's prohibitions show us the minimum, not the maximum level of obedience.

One such minimum is the Bible's disapproval of usury or lending at interest. The maximum goes much further. In the same breath as the command to love our enemies, Jesus tells us to lend without expecting to get even the principal back (Luke 6:34-35). Twice he goes further and advises selling one's possessions (Luke 12:33 and 18:22). At the very least, these passages should stimulate vigilance in any church that strives to be Bible-centered and lives in prosperous times. In many cases, they should be a source of positive embarrassment.

Sometimes Christians find themselves in complicated situations where the choice between good and evil is not clear. Many economic questions are of this sort, especially when no effort is made to face them as a community. But the first question before every Christian is clear: Am I ready to trust in God's care sufficiently to forsake all and follow Christ?

8

Nonconformity and the Nation[1]

Abraham is described in the book of Hebrews as a hero of faith because he obeyed God's command to leave the highly civilized nation in which he lived, to become a wanderer, and to remain a wanderer even in the land that God had promised him. The whole theme of the "faith chapter" (Hebrews 11) is not that faith means believing the unlikely or the impossible, but that faith means trusting God's promises enough to obey God by being, if necessary, a misfit. Abel, Noah, and Abraham inaugurate the line of those of whom it is said, "All of these died in faith . . . They confessed that they were strangers and foreigners on the earth, for people who speak in this way make it clear that they are seeking a homeland. . . . they desire a better country, that is, a heavenly one. Therefore God is not ashamed to be called their God" (vv. 13-14, 16). The list of all these faithful ones, whose obedience made them out of place in a disobedient world, concludes with the statement that "the world was not worthy" of them (v. 38).

This does not mean that the Bible considers these heroes to have been extraordinarily good in all respects, with none of the failings of ordinary people. The opposite is true. Because

---

1. "Nonconformity and the Nation," *Christian Living* (February 1955): 8–9, 25, 33.

they were weak and fallible people, their example calls us also to obey God in the face of the world's disapproval and our apparent failure.

It is worth noting that both the list of heroes in the "faith chapter" and the sketch of Israel's history given by Stephen before the Sanhedrin (Acts 7) stop with the beginnings of the political kingdom under David. The Jewish national kingdom of the Old Testament is not considered by the New Testament to have been the fulfillment of God's promise to Abraham. Christ himself continually resisted the tendency of his contemporaries to understand his kingdom as a matter of Jewish national loyalty. He was consistently misunderstood by his disciples, by the crowds of Jerusalem, and by the Romans who put him to death as a Zealot. Thus Christ himself crowns the line of obedient misfits of whom the world is unworthy, and his obedience is our example and command. "Servants are not greater than their master" (John 13:16).

Pagan condemnation of the early Christians followed the same pattern. No one cared that they had a different God or that they believed in the resurrection or in salvation from sins. The Roman Empire tolerated all sorts of belief, all forms of worship, and any kind of behavior. They were not an offense because of any particular way of acting or dressing or worshiping, but because of their obedience to God. Such obedience, which became visible at various points depending on circumstances, made it clear that they were not good loyal citizens of the world that surrounded them.

In the sixteenth century, the Anabaptists drew upon themselves the wrath of the world because of their obedience. The particular issues—their refusal of infant baptism and of the oath in conformity with specific New Testament teaching—were only symptoms of their deeper refusal. That deeper refusal entailed cutting themselves off from the people and nation for which both the loyalty oath and infant baptism were the religious underpinning. Their offense was not so much false doctrine as social and political disloyalty. This is why the martyrs complained, "The world has become too small for us."[2] Their devotion to the kingdom of God and their love for

---

2. Yoder is referring to a statement that a group of seventy Anabaptists wrote after Leonhard Schoener was executed for being an Anabaptist. They

all people, even their enemies, made them unreliable citizens of the city-states and provinces of medieval Europe.

What must be noticed in all these cases is that the persecution of the faithful did not come from the irreligious, but from the very religious. The Babylonian city that Abraham left, Canaan and Egypt where he lived as a stranger, the Israelite kingdoms that persecuted the prophets, the Roman Empire that tortured Christians, and the sixteenth-century Protestant governments that oppressed the early Anabaptists were all very religious cultures. In fact, that was the trouble. The issue is not between religion and irreligion, nor even between Christian orthodoxy and false doctrine. The issue is between the true faith which, by obedience, causes a break with the world, and false religion which, though its doctrine might be orthodox, confirms and sanctions the unity of fallen society through religious observance. This unity of fallen society, similar to true faith, also demands sacrificial obedience (the soldier is the best example). But this is an obedience in the interests of national unity, not in the loving service of enemy and friend alike.

A striking Old Testament illustration of this difference can be seen in 1 Kings 22. Micaiah, son of Imlah, the true prophet of the Lord, was interested in obedience when he condemned the plans of Ahab and Jehoshaphat, the kings of Israel and Judah. He was overruled by four hundred prophets of the official church (also worshipers of the true God) who said, "Go up . . . and triumph; the LORD will give it into the hand of the king" (1 Kings 22:12).

Religion as creating national unity

We have discussed in a previous chapter the danger of a crusading mentality. So our concern here is not so much that way

---

said, in part: "The believers have here been hanged on trees, strangled, cut in pieces, drowned secretly and openly; not only men, but also women and maidens have testified here to the faith that Jesus Christ is the truth and the only way to eternal life. . . . Still the world is not at rest, but rages like a madman, and forges lies against us. They cease not to burn and kill. They make the world too small for us." See Thieleman J. Van Braght, *The Martyrs' Mirror*, 15th ed. (Scottdale, PA: Herald Press, 1987), 426.

of thinking, with its wrongly pessimistic view of the enemy and its wrongly optimistic view of one's own innocence. Our present concern is the idea that religion is a binding force that creates national unity, instead of a demand for higher obedience that brings "not peace but a sword" (Matthew 10:34).

For a modern example of the same attitude to religion that we see in Ahab and Jehoshaphat, any modern nation may be chosen. Americans might well choose the United States, which is no exception. In fact, the way in which many aspects of American life have been influenced by Christian teachings makes it a special temptation for Americans to feel that their nationalistic loyalty is willed by God. This is especially so when the leading political opponent of America is a nation whose leaders are believed to have opposed Christianity.

To observe this "national religion" in American life we must remember that there can be a national religion without a state church. All that is needed is for people to think that religion is first of all a support of national unity and well being. The term *religion* is often preferred to *Christianity*. When the term *Christian* or even *Protestant* is used, it seldom refers to any particularly evangelical doctrine or way of life. More often it refers to a religion accepted by the large majority, which assures them that God is not so much a Lord who demands obedience as a handyman who is available whenever we need help.

Is America a Christian nation?

Some Christians feel that America is a Christian nation especially charged with a divine calling because the president pronounced a prayer before his inauguration and took the oath of office with his hand on two Bibles. Here the judgment of the disciple will not be so hasty. On one hand, we must appreciate the sincerity and the honesty of the leaders of our present government, which is not entirely independent of the fact that both president and vice president come from peace church backgrounds.[3] Yet at the same time we should

---

3. President Dwight Eisenhower's mother, Ida Elizabeth Stover Eisenhower, grew up River Brethren, a group that broke away from the

note that there was nothing specifically Christian about that prayer. Its concern was the unity and prosperity of the nation, which is assumed to be the same as "right." We find in it no repentance or acknowledgment of standing before God's judgment, no expression of love for the enemy or separation from the world, no submission of national self-interest under a higher moral law, and no mention of the name of Christ. A Jew, Freemason, or Muslim could pray the same prayer.

A lengthy article on "The President's Religious Faith" in a leading religious journal supports the same conclusion.[4] The conscientious submission to government as God's instrument and the honor we owe to "kings" should not change our refusal to identify Christianity with the nation's religion.

This identification becomes far more serious when the attempt is made to claim that American nationalism is sanctioned not only by religion in general, but by evangelical Protestantism. Such attitudes exist and create a strange mixture of biblical and nationalistic ideas. This was evident in a ceremony dedicating the United States to the defense of "Seven Freedoms" defined in the twenty-third Psalm.[5] It would be hard to imagine anything more dangerous for faith than this confusion of motives. In reality, this is the same thing we saw in 1 Kings 22. Instead of seeing God's judgment on one's own nation, the sins of the enemy are magnified and God is called upon to bless one nation at the expense of others. Even the Israelites, God's own people, were wrong to expect such a one-sided blessing. In the case of the United States, God's judgment may be upon the unrestrained private exploitation of natural resources and on the use of restraints on trade and immigration to keep this wealth for a few.

Mennonites in the late eighteenth century over the proper form of baptism. They have remained a pacifist church. The largest branch today is the Brethren in Christ. Richard Nixon, Eisenhower's vice president, grew up in a Quaker church.

4. See Paul Hutchinson, "The President's Religious Faith," *Life* (March 22, 1954): 151–62,167–70.

5. Yoder is referring to Eisenhower's and Nixon's endorsement of the 1953 "Declaration of Freedom" that the National Association of Evangelicals drew up to defend "seven freedoms" based on Psalm 23 and to reaffirm America's religious heritage. See "The Seven Freedoms," *Time* (July 13, 1953): 76.

Nationalism, not war, is our greatest temptation

In the cases of Abraham, the early church, and the Anabaptists, we saw that the reason for the break between church and world was their full response to God's call to discipleship and the love of Christ. It is noteworthy that fundamentalist nationalists, who vocally favor the Bible when it is a question of making biblical authority a subject of quarrel, show little interest in New Testament discipleship, either in nonresistance or in its judgment that state officials are "least esteemed by the church." In fact, such groups attach an exaggerated importance to military and government officials and their professions of faith. This is so even when such professions are not evangelical in content and involve chiefly the desire for a higher power's help in carrying out a political or military agenda.

Precisely because the American government leaves room for the specific act of refusing military service, often making that refusal easier than military service, the temptation is great to forget that the real evil is not in the act of bearing arms. The real evil is the whole attitude of nationalism and the willingness to attach one's loyalty to something less than the kingdom of God with its impartial love of neighbor. If our conscientious objection leaves us just as materialistic, just as anticommunistic, just as willing to accept a one-sided view of world affairs, just as "at home" in business and the community, just as accustomed to thinking our way of doing things is right, then our objection to military service is not "conscientious" at all, but inconsistent and legalistic.

Following Christ without indifference or compromise

One attempt to negotiate the Christian's relation to the government has been that of "withdrawal," as if having no interest in current events makes Christians more faithful to their heavenly calling. Like the doctrine of Christians who want to have no creed but the Bible and end up with wrong doctrines, the attempt to have no political or social position really means having a rightist position. Such a position is true to the example of neither the Old Testament prophets nor the early Anabaptists, to say nothing of Jesus' own judgment on specific social and political abuses.

The contrary attempt, whose motto is "responsibility," works for justice in society with whatever methods are necessary. Many individuals with high ideals have accomplished much that is commendable in public service. Yet there comes a point when a choice must be made between unqualified love of neighbor and unqualified national loyalty. Of the two alternatives, one means leaving government service and the other means leaving Christ or at least taking part of one's life away from him.

The Christian path between indifference and compromise is a difficult one to trace and an unpopular one to follow, but it is the way of Christ. Christians have not always had the wisdom to find, or the courage to take, the path "in but not of the world." Some have stayed too far "out of the world" and others too far "in and of." Here I submit six elements of what it would mean to properly follow Christ in this respect:

1. Insofar as a government respects its God-given function of "punishing evil and encouraging good," the Christian will commend its faithfulness and submit to its regulation and taxation for conscience's sake. In this sense it is legitimate to honor those officials who have done this in the past and even to prefer America to some other countries with less conscientious governments.

2. Insofar as a government oversteps the conditions of this divine authorization, by punishing good and encouraging evil, the Christian will prophetically condemn this injustice and refuse to support it. This judgment applies to war in any sense, except a strictly limited police action. That a Christian should support war (even to the point of paying taxes and performing alternative service[6]) is not as clearly stated in the

---

6. By "alternative service" Yoder is referring to official exemption from military service during World War II, in which peace church members who were drafted could serve in the Civilian Public Service (CPS) labor camps run by churches instead of the military or going to prison. This was a contentious issue in pacifist circles. The American Friends Service Committee, for example, withdrew from the arrangement. Mennonite leadership, by contrast, supported the program as a sign of Mennonite patriotism and nonresistance. For an overview of the

New Testament as some think. The Roman forces in Palestine, which Jesus and Paul accepted as part of the situation, were not used for international war, but for a policing function. It is one thing to accept the reality of local officers committed to keeping order and preserving peace; it is another to endorse the kind of mass killing that happens in warfare for a variety of reasons. It is regrettable that Christian witness to government has come in the past mostly from Christians without a fully biblical orientation about such matters.

3. Such witness to government should express the Christian's criticism of specific injustices in the state's behavior or elsewhere in social life. This is the true form of the church's responsibility for the social order. It is the call to repentance and "works worthy of repentance." Its biblical expression is, "Do you not know that we are to judge angels" (1 Corinthians 6:3). The term *angels* here (as in Romans 8:38 and 1 Peter 3:22) refers not vaguely to heavenly beings in general, but to those spiritual forces standing behind worldly authorities, as the parallel in verse 2 indicates. The church's mission in the world is not only saving souls, but also proclaiming God's just and merciful will to the powers that be (Ephesians 3:10). Expressing this kind of judgment would not be "getting involved in politics." It would not require office holding and would sometimes forbid it. It is the path of Christian discipleship.

4. Insofar as an unjust state attacks the Christian unfairly, the Christian should both condemn the injustice and submit to it out of love. Here we follow the example of Christ who submitted to unjust condemnation and execution at the hands of the Roman authorities (cf. 1 Peter 2). Injustice toward others should be denounced and resisted by any means consistent with love for the agents of government.

---

history and issues surrounding CPS, see Perry Bush, *Two Kingdoms, Two Loyalties* (Baltimore, MD: John Hopkins University Press, 1998), 56–128.

5. Insofar as the state undertakes activities unrelated to the police function and aimed at the common good, Christians whose vocation calls them to such public service may serve the state just as they might serve under any local agency. They must do so, however, with the same limits of faithfulness where conscience draws the line. Education, roads, and public health are examples of such fields of service.

6. If the state thinks that by its planning and direction of society and economy it can achieve an ideal social order, the Christian's witness is a reminder of how human sinfulness corrupts even the best of plans. Christians will therefore oppose the concentration of power in the hands of a few and will prefer forms of government and social order that, without guaranteeing perfect justice, provide the most effective checks and balances against individual ambitions. Christians will be dubious about the values of either "free enterprise" or the "planned economy" as a matter of economic doctrine. Both are subject to the same flaw—human sinfulness—and Christians will be most interested in workable ways of keeping planners and free entrepreneurs from taking advantage of their power.

It has often happened that American missionaries and relief workers when serving abroad have felt more at home with other Americans while there—be they of diplomatic, military, or commercial circles—than with native Christians. This demonstrates the degree to which the unquestioned adoption of a way of life and thought hinders the real Christian cause in the world far more significantly than the language barrier. The conformity of missionaries to the world, in the form of loyalty to their home country and its culture, is a significant reason, if not the major reason, why doors in the Far East are closing to Christian missions.

"I have given them your word, and the world has hated them because they do not belong to the world, just as I do not belong to the world" (John 17:14). There is no difference between nonconformity to the world and conformity to Christ. Both mean a positive obedience to God's higher love.

Such obedience puts the Christian out of place, a stranger, and a source of irritation. The Christian is not "at home" in the world because he or she bears a message of judgment and mercy from the one whom the world flees. It is up to us to ask whether this is the impression we give by our own, our neighbors', and our nation's economic, social, and political attitudes toward life.

9

Time and the Christian[1]

One of the characteristics of our age is the fabulous development of ways to spend our leisure time. With the continued shortening of the work week, the term *leisure*, once applicable only to an elite class or to the worker's Sunday, has come to include almost half of many people's waking time.

There is no shortage of industries set up to provide "entertainment." Sometimes this term refers to culturally valuable ways of spending time. More often the time is simply "killed," leaving the "entertained" only the poorer for their expenditure. And so we may observe that parallel to people's effort to have more time freed from the demands of work is a rising tide of effort to escape boredom through nonproductive work or distraction. Being left alone with oneself is something the modern person can't stand for long.

Making the most of time

In the second half of Paul's letter to the Ephesians, we find two exhortations to nonconformity: "You must no longer live as the Gentiles live" (4:17) and "once you were darkness, but now in the Lord you are light" (5:8). One of the commands

---

1. "Time and the Christian," *Christian Living* (March 1955): 15.

that define this nonconformity for us is "Be careful then how you live . . . making the most of the time, because the days are evil" (5:15-16). Coupled with the call to "work for the night is coming,"[2] this gives us a clue that our attitude regarding time is one of the ways Christians will be different.

One of the proverbs that seem to non-Americans most representative of the American mentality is the well-worn phrase, "Time is money." The best thing Americans can do with time is to assign financial value. "Money is time" would be a more profound statement; but the real reason time should matter for us is not because it has financial value, but because our time has been entrusted to us by God. In redeeming us at a great price (remember that *redeem* means "to buy"), God became owner not only of our bodies, but also of our time and money. Our stewardship applies equally to all three.

Time means an opportunity to glorify God. Its passing is the procession of openings for service and witness. Each opening passes us by only once from the fluid future toward the frozen past. No moment will come by again. With every one of them our total reserve of opportunities for service is shortened as our past accumulates.

This is why Christians take their lives seriously. In pagan religions, neither one's sins nor one's good works can be very important. Time just goes around in circles without any meaning. Since life has no special direction or destination, the only problem is how to spend it in the least boring way. But the Christian knows that time does have meaning, that it only happens once, and that every second matters. The Christian looks back to the unique works of creation and reconciliation, and forward to the once-and-for-all consummation of the kingdom and the judgment already seen in Christ. All of this is bound to the chain of events in time, and Christians know that there is a vital relationship between communion with God and the use we make of every minute entrusted to us. Standing accountable for the lives we have received, we live constantly in the awareness of life's inexorable trickling past. Not that the Christian fears coming death—perfect love casts out all fear (1 John 4:18). But perfect love also seeks perfect discipleship.

---

2. Yoder is referencing a hymn by this title, which is based on John 9:4.

The Christian's attitude will not be one of fearful tension, but the calm sincere purposefulness of a worker with a task to do in limited time.

Time is what life is made of. "Killing time" is less visible and less violent, but in its own way it is a kind of murder or suicide. It is just as final in its destruction. So the Christian will have something definite to say about any loitering, any disregard for schedules, any entertainment, any conversation, any hobby, and any travel whose sole significance is that it makes the hours go by. It is not as if such things are in themselves evil, forbidden, or harmful. But we will have something to say about them because we haven't time to waste.

It would be possible to speak of two kinds of Christian use of time. One is productive activity, like farming or manufacturing. The other is religious, like preaching or praying. Such a distinction does as much harm as good. In fact, to reserve the term "full-time Christian service" for the latter is to express an attitude that is foreign to the gospel. Plowing is, or should be, as religious as praying. Bible reading is, or should be, just as labor intensive as road building. Whatever activity full-time Christians turn to is, or should be, worthy of all their attention and ability, and subject to critical evaluation as a case of time-redeeming stewardship.

Godly rest versus modern vacations

Where then do we find time for rest, for recreation, for vacationing? There was a time when, in rural areas, vacationing was unknown and the workday stretched from dawn to dark. Now the ease of modern living has made the annual two to four weeks off seem to many as indispensable as their deep freezers and late model automobiles. Rightly so, for vacations and deep freezers alike are signs of a standard of living above that of the rest of the world. The fact that many live without them does not make them wrong, but even less does the fact that we would not like to live without them make them right. The question is always the same: Is this the most effective investment of my gifts that, here and now, I can make for the glory of God and the service of my neighbor? That vacations have become the accepted norm does not make them wrong for the Christian, but neither does it make them right.

If we need to learn that a change of activities can be for people in many kinds of work a way to rest, to heighten one's effectiveness for service, to restore one's physical capacities, and to broaden one's knowledge and understanding of others, then we need to remember that much recreation and many kinds of vacation do not have this effect. Furthermore, when the doctor prescribes a change of scenery, a complete rest, "getting away from it all," for a person whose interest in life is really self-centered boredom, that does not mean that Christians who realize that everything we do is full-time Christian service will need the same kind of release. The body may need rest, the mind may seek new frontiers, but such people have no "need" to get away from their self or their vocation.

It is no accident that the need for vacations has arisen in an age that no longer honors Sunday. We need not be Puritans or advocates of sabbatarian legalism to recognize that in the weekly cycle of work and worship we have both the divine authorization for legitimate rest and a more natural way of meeting that need than the annual hurried trip to somewhere else.

The insistence that all our time belongs to God means that we should work hard. It does not mean we should be working all the time. It means that our rest, our conversation, and our study must all be seen as ways to serve God. Our "free time" is no more our own than our work hours. For both alike we are accountable to God who is their real owner.

One life per person is all we have been given. Hiding from that sobering truth, people seek at once to lengthen life by avoiding work and to shorten it with useless diversions. If we belong to Christ, let that belonging be seen in our stewardship of this unique pleasure and in our willingness to pour it out where love demands. Jesus once let his vacation plans drop when needy people sought him out (Mark 6:30-44). May we, too, be known as people "on call," whose lives belong to Christ and to the least of his kin.

10

Discipleship and Self-Assertion[1]

Human nature is such that people seek self-expression. The desire for power and the search for wealth and enjoyment are all indicators of humanity's deep craving for self-affirmation. Yet we live in a world where no one can always be or have what he or she wants. The fulfillment of one's wishes is frustrated by convention, by law, by limited means, or by collision with the wishes of others.

The field of psychiatry has grown rapidly in response to this situation. The psychiatrist attempts to adjust people to their frustrations. He or she helps them find ways to satisfy the craving for self-affirmation in spite of life's obstacles. The ideal personality, as portrayed in literature and movies, as cultivated through education, and as admired in successful executives, is one whose self-affirmation is disciplined, channeled, and above all, effective.

The nonconformity passages in Ephesians look at this character trait differently: "Be subject to one another out of reverence for Christ" (Ephesians 5:21). The apostle goes on

---

1. "Discipleship and Self-Assertion," *Christian Living* (April 1955): 28–29.

to apply this instruction to relationships between husbands and wives, parents and children, masters and slaves. The length of this passage suggests that this is one of the crucial ways we demonstrate that we are not of this world.

"Reverence for Christ" is the reason we are subject to one another. Just as the way to serve Christ is to meet the concrete needs of "the least of these my brethren," so also the way to revere Christ is to honor the person, the personality, the will of our fellow Christian and neighbor. Just as God's love for us was triumphantly revealed in the humility and obedience of Christ, so will its manifestation be in our time the humility and submissiveness of the disciple (Philippians 2). Nothing was more unexpected than finding humility at the heart of God's representative.

It was part of the "scandal" that kept many Jews and Greeks from faith in Paul's time and it continues to mark the border between discipleship and the religions of prestige in our own time. Learning to follow the way of Christ demands a spiritual shifting of gears that is never really completed. "Let the same mind be in you that was in Christ Jesus" (Philippians 2:5). This means that the Christian life is a process of seeking to live up to the definition of a Christian. A Christian, by definition, is a copy of Christ's self-effacing love. We are called to become that. This is why Paul first proclaims in Colossians 3:3, "You have died" (by definition), and then instructs us in verse 5 to "put to death" (a call to fulfill the definition).

Church discipline and self-assertion

The question of church discipline or, more broadly, the biblical way of settling differences, is one place where such a spiritual gear-shifting is needed. We often feel that the procedure outlined in Matthew 18 ("Go and point out the fault when the two of you are alone . . . [then] take one or two others . . . [then] tell it to the church.") provides the machinery by which one may get even with one's adversary—a clear expression of the will to dominate. Yet the clearly taught intention of the whole procedure is indicated by Christ: "If the member listens to you, you have regained that one" (Matthew 18:15). The intention is not domination or exclusion but reconciliation. Even church discipline must come within the redemptive purpose of the Christian life.

If in some circles the practice of church discipline has fallen into disuse, it is easy to trace the reason to a concept of discipline that was more authoritarian than redemptive. The early Anabaptists were aware of this danger. They coupled their insistence on discipline with Jesus' word that "the rulers of the Gentiles lord it over them, and their great ones are tyrants over them. *It will not be so among you*; but whoever wishes to be great among you must be your servant . . . just as the Son of Man came not to be served but to serve" (Matthew 20:25-28). Again the passage relates discipleship and nonconformity. The alternatives are to do as the Gentiles do or to do as Christ did. One alternative means following Christ; the other means self-assertion.

Authority in the church

So it is that our nonconformity must find its expression in the major areas of human interaction—in the family, at the place of work, in the work of the church—wherever human beings come together the choice must be made between attempts to dominate and attempts to serve. The sad lesson of Christian history is that even in the church, even in "evangelical" churches, far too often there have been signs of this particular kind of worldliness. In fact, the process of development that led to the Roman Catholic Church was largely just that. It was a gradually increasing domination assumed first by the bishops and then by some bishops over others (archbishops), in imitation of the efficient administrative setup of the Roman Empire.

The difference between the pomp and worldly authority of the bishops and the pope and the sacrificial humility of Christ was one of the strongest arguments of Reformers and Anabaptists in the sixteenth century. Yet only the Anabaptists saw that the answer was not a patching up or reforming of the old authoritarian church organization, which continued to impose its sacraments upon every European. Rather, it was a new beginning of fraternal fellowship among those who chose freely the service of the Master. They spoke no longer of "bishop" and "priest," but of "elders" and "servants."

Our word *minister* has the same meaning, in origin if not always in use. It indicates that the real authority in the church should not be its preacher (as the term *Reverend* suggests), but the Spirit-led fellowship of believers, each submitting in love to the will of others.

True individuality

Let no one think that this sort of Christian submissiveness would bring to pass a sheeplike uniformity of people without backbones or individuality. Humanity is so made that self-expression and individuality are fruitful only in submission to God and neighbor. Without that submission, individuality becomes eccentricity and self-expression pure egoism. Nothing is more boring and less individual than the way in which, hoping to be different, everyone adopts the latest dress fad, the latest slang, the latest entertainment idol, and the latest form of disrespect for manners and morals. True individualists know how to relate creatively to tradition, authority, and family. They relate not in blind indifference or aimless rebellion, but with Christian concern for those whom God has given them to love.

Christ's submission to Judaism and to Roman authority did not mean approval of their sins or lack of personality and critical capacity. It was simply love. That kind of love didn't fit in the world then and it still doesn't now. Yet it is such love that Peter writes about when he uses the verb *be subject* four times (1 Peter 2:13, 18; 3:1, 5; 5:5) and then says, "to this you have been called" (1 Peter 2:21).

As always, the call is to discipleship that makes a difference. That difference is the willingness to give oneself in love to the fellowship. How we answer is up to us.

11

Let Your Yes Be Yes[1]

Ever since Abel, God's way of working has been to ask people to be different. Noah had to make himself look silly building a floatable barn on dry land, and the line goes on from him through Abraham to the chosen people. The whole history of the Hebrews can be understood as God's effort to bring the nation to understand that it should not be like other nations. Sometimes they wished they had stayed in Egypt, sometimes they insisted on having a king and an army like other peoples, and sometimes they copied the religion of their Canaanite neighbors. Ever and again God, through the prophets, had to drum into them that they were called to be different. "You shall be holy, for I the LORD your God am holy" (Leviticus 19:2) was the command ever since the exodus that made Israel a nation. *Holy* here does not primarily mean morally pure; it means separated, set aside, consecrated.

That they were separated from the world in order to be faithful to God began to sink into the Jews' consciousness about the time of their exile. From then on, the imitation of other peoples falls into the background and is replaced by the opposite error of thinking that God's favor toward

1. "Let Your Yes Be Yes," *Christian Living* (May 1955): 20–21.

them was something they possessed by heredity or earned by keeping the Law.

As mistaken as this idea was, it still had at its core the truth that God's people must be different. This was recognized by Jesus himself. He gave, as a reason for not being anxious, the fact that the Gentiles are worried about what to eat and drink (Matthew 6:32).

Truthfulness and nonconformity

One of the first points at which God began the moral education of the Jewish people had to do with truthfulness. The oath in the name of a divinity was, at that time, highly respected as a safeguard against falsehood. It was believed that the god somehow would intervene to prevent or punish the breaking of an oath. How well this worked depended on whether the fear of the god in question was greater than the temptation to bail out. Often it was not.

The belief in the one true God changed all this. Once the Hebrews were separated and belonged to God in a special way, there was no question whether the fear of Yahweh took precedence over the urge to break a promise. An oath that God had been asked to sanction became an object of God's own faithfulness. To break it is to offend God's honor. So it is that the first commandment after those dealing with the worship of Yahweh alone is the one against the false oath. To "take the name of the LORD your God in vain" means just that (Exodus 20:7 ESV). It means calling upon God to ratify a promise that one does not intend to keep. The application of this commandment to cursing is not false, but it is not the primary meaning.

A way can be found around any rule. This one was no exception. To avoid the seriousness of swearing by the name of Yahweh, one could swear by another of Yahweh's names, by the temple, or by heaven. This had the same ceremonial value in giving the oath a kind of religious sanction, but it was hoped that legally it would not be quite so binding. Thus the whole process of swearing, originally meant to protect the truth, became an instrument for further falsehood.

Jesus solved the question in a radical way. Instead of asking for a new sincerity in the fulfillment of oaths, he swept away the whole system. "Do not swear at all" (Matthew 5:34). The use of an oath to guarantee the trustworthiness of a statement or promise is a tacit admission that, if there were no oath, a lie might not be out of place. Once again, as in so many other realms, an Old Testament commandment, which in itself is "holy and just and good" (Romans 7:12), and which should have set the Hebrews apart from other nations by their faithfulness, had turned out to be inadequate. It had even become a legitimation of the opposite of what was intended.

Since the Jewish people had failed to become the holy, different folk that God wanted, its place was taken by the church, a new creation, a people belonging especially to God. The difference from the pagans, which the Jews never brought about in the right way, is now expected of the Christians. As was the case in the Old Testament, so again in the New a major part of that nonconformity has to do with *truth*. We see it among the Jewish church of Acts, where the only disorder within the church that is reported in detail is the falsehood of Ananias and Sapphira. Likewise we find it in Gentile Christianity, where the apostle Paul had to do for new converts the job of moral education that had taken centuries under the Law. Paul writes to the young churches,

> Put to death, therefore, whatever in you is earthly: fornication, impurity, passion, evil desire, and greed (which is idolatry). On account of these the wrath of God is coming on those who are disobedient. These are the ways you also once followed, when you were living that life. But now you must get rid of all such things—anger, wrath, malice, slander, and abusive language from your mouth. Do not lie to one another, seeing that you have stripped off the old self with its practices and have clothed yourselves with the new self, which is being renewed in knowledge according to the image of its creator. (Colossians 3:5-10)

Here the nonconformity of truthfulness is seen from two sides. Looking backward, it means breaking with the old way of life, which was under God's judgment. The devil is "a liar and the father of lies" (John 8:44), so lying belongs to his children. Looking forward, truthfulness means "putting on a new nature" that points to God's own nature and finds its renewal in being recognizably modeled after the Creator. *Truth* is a synonym for Christ (John 14:6) and for the gospel (1 Peter 1:22). Thus, as should always be the case, our non-conformity to the world is defined by our conformity to "the Father of lights, with whom there is no variation," who "in fulfillment of his own purpose . . . gave us birth by the word of truth, so that we would become a kind of first fruits of his creatures" (James 1:17-18).

At another place, in the same connection with the change that defines the Christian, Paul writes, "Put away your former way of life . . . and be renewed in the spirit of your minds, and . . . clothe yourselves with the new self, created according to the likeness of God . . . putting away falsehood, let us all speak the truth to our neighbors, for we are members of one another" (Ephesians 4:22-25). In many ways this passage exactly parallels the other, but it goes deeper into the meaning of truth or falsehood for human interaction. "Members of one another" is a stronger expression than we realize. "Member" has nothing to do with the modern idea of "membership" as a loose sort of voluntary affiliation that can be taken up or chopped at will. A "member" is part of the physical body— the hand (Matthew 5:29), the tongue (James 3:5), the foot, the ear, and the eye (1 Corinthians 12). Paul is using here one of his favorite and most pointed images for the organic unity of all believers, not only with Christ but also with each other.

A moment's meditation will convince anyone how profoundly true it is that falsehood introduces into social relations or Christian fellowship a disharmony as serious as an amputation. The effort expended to check falsehood in school, in bookkeeping, in tax declaration, and at border crossings is only a symbol of the poisonous effect that a lack of confidence can have for the most elementary forms of human community. Nothing can undermine more the day-to-day meaningfulness of life than the necessity of suspecting, doubting, checking, and disbelieving that arises when one's neighbors can't be trusted.

Uncomfortable truths

Truthfulness is uncomfortable too, but in another way. Whereas with falsehood one can defend one's privacy, holding others at arm's length so to speak, the commitment to honesty drops all defenses. This is what makes possible the depth of Christian fellowship. "Members of one another" are no longer at arm's length. When there is something to hide, such close contact gives one a naked feeling. So it is that most civilizations, especially those with a high degree of stability and a dense population, develop a complex framework of slight falsehoods, exaggerations, or embellishments known as "manners." ("What a pleasure it is to meet you!") Some things one must always say, other things one must never say. Only children risk creating embarrassing situations by saying what they think.

But Jesus told us to be like children. This does not mean that politeness or decent consideration for the other's feelings is wrong. They are necessary expressions of love. But the difference between considerate love and insincere artificiality remains, and the Christian must not lose it from view.

One of the most fundamental expressions of Christian love within the church, and the one most different from the ways of the world, is the way we are instructed to deal with our misunderstandings and disagreements. The Bible doesn't expect us to avoid having differences, even with fellow Christians, but it tells us clearly how to settle them. The tactful way to approach such a problem is to "let it blow over" or to talk about it with one's friends but not to seek directly a personal understanding with the offender. As considerate as this may seem, in that it avoids going over the distasteful past and raising questions of right and wrong, this attitude really makes fellow members (in the strong sense of the word) into things. It treats them as a problem in psychology rather than as fellow Christians, pretending to forget without having forgiven.

The Christian alternative to this kind of mistaken strategy is not only clear in Matthew 5:23-24 and 18:15. We may also suppose that in the two passages we have quoted, Paul was thinking not only of outright deceit and gross evasion, but also of the discreet distance and tendency to discuss such problems with those other than the person in question. "Speak the truth with his neighbor" means "don't go around talking to other people about it." Since both passages speak in the same breath about getting over anger and forgiving as we have been forgiven, this interpretation is quite normal. This thought recurs so often in the New Testament that we must think of the reestablishment of unity and familial openness in fellowship as an essential part of the life of the church and of nonconformity.

There was a time when Mennonites gave their lives because of their refusal to swear. There was a time when a Mennonite tenant's word was worth more to a landlord than another person's sworn contract. Whether or not we agree with those who feel that those times are past, we must admit that there are few more potent examples of the way in which nonconformity can be a positive witness to the meaning of Christian faith. If we understand the question as a matter of legalism, we soon get bogged down in borderline questions as to what is a lie, as to white lies, and as to not telling the whole truth. But if we seek to conform our lives to the pattern of Christ whose whole purpose was to reveal openly and proclaim God's own being, we shall rediscover that "if we walk in the light as he himself is in the light, we have fellowship with one another . . . Whoever loves a brother or sister lives in the light, and in such a person there is no cause for stumbling" (1 John 1:7; 2:10).

12

Love Unlimited[1]

Humans are at heart kind and sociable. Such a statement may seem unorthodox to Christians who believe that human nature is so corrupted and distorted that only a divine miracle can enable a person to do God's will. Yet no degree of corruption can uproot from the human heart the leaning toward unselfishness and service that the Creator put there. Even criminals have a sort of morality among themselves, and the most brutal person can still be touched by pity and will feel good after an occasional act of gentleness or even sacrifice.

It would thus be far from the truth to claim love as a specifically Christian virtue. It would be wrongheaded to assume that the originality of Jesus' ministry was his teaching that we should love our neighbors, or to suggest that only Christians really love. It would be good for Christians to meditate more often, both in the interest of humility and as an aid to understanding the world for which they have a message, on the amount of love, unselfishness, and willingness to sacrifice and serve that non-Christians often exhibit. Such a meditation would make us aware of how we might recognize and speak to the kernel of goodness in

---

1. "Love Unlimited," *Christian Living* (June 1955): 24–25.

every person. It would help us realize how much more than human goodness is involved in the love that Jesus asks of his followers.

Jesus affirms that all people are capable of love: "For if you love those who love you, what reward do you have? Do not even the tax collectors do the same? And if you greet only your brothers and sisters, what more are you doing than others? Do not even the Gentiles do the same?" (Matthew 5:46-47). His argument takes as its starting point that his followers will somehow be different from the "pagans" in such a way as to deserve "reward." Again, we are told in Scripture that being different is part of what it means to be Christian. It is worth our while to ask once more what this difference is. This time we focus on what is different about our love.

Human love is related to human nearness. The mother loves and will sacrifice for her child. The father will protect his family. "You then, who are evil, know how to give good gifts to your children" (Matthew 7:11), is the way Jesus observed that parental love is normal in any society. Likewise the club, the lodge, the neighborhood, or the nation may be the framework in which love of neighbor is practiced. One of the characteristics of human love is that it is limited; that it applies to some people, inside some group, and not, at least not to the same extent, to other people, outside the group. If a conflict of interests arises, this love will take sides and will choose one group above another, its own group over the opposing one. This pattern reveals such love to be, deep down inside, a subtle form of selfishness.

The lawyer who asked Jesus, "Who is my neighbor?" had the same idea in mind (Luke 10:29). He wanted a handy rule to tell him just how far love had to go. He wanted to know who it would be okay not to love, or at least to love less. We often forget that the parable of the "good Samaritan" was not given as a general teaching that we should do good—everybody knows that—but as a direct answer to the question, "Who is my neighbor?" When we remember how Samaritans were despised in Jesus' time, we see that the answer Jesus gave by naming the Samaritan was the same one he gave earlier saying, "Love your enemies" (Luke 6:27, 35). In other words, the limits of group, nation, and religion are not the frontiers of our love. The refusal to let our love be stopped by a border—be it of race, creed, or human sympathy—will be the measure of our Christian nonconformity.

Jesus defines love for the Christian

When we say "love," we should not forget, despite all that the world around us would have us believe, that love is not the way we feel inside. We sometimes encounter the claim that it is possible to love our enemies at the same time as killing them, to love members of another race without associating with them, or to love people of another class while refusing to treat them as equals. This kind of stance is only possible if one thinks that love is some kind of well-meaning feeling that involves no personal commitment to a way of acting.

Christians must start with a far different definition of love. Our definition of love is Christ, who sacrificed his divine privileges, became human, even a slave, and gave himself so completely to his fellow people, friends or enemies, as to die at their hands (Philippians 2). Love is not a vague hope that things will go well for everyone (James 2). It is an action that assumes the responsibility and costs of *doing* good.

Not only does the love of Christ refuse to stop at national borders, it also refuses to accept the family as a special focus. "I have come to set a man against his father, and a daughter against her mother . . . and one's foes will be members of one's own household. Whoever loves father or mother . . . son or daughter more than me is not worthy of me" (Matthew 10:35-37). This does not mean, solely, that religious values take precedence over family values. Jesus tells us elsewhere that the way to love him is to love "the least of these" (Matthew 25). What he means to say is quite concrete: "Whoever loves those of their own household more than the least of my disciples—those who are hungry, naked, sick, or in prison—is not worthy of me." Jesus does not deny the duty, even the primary duty, to care for one's relatives when they are in need. The responsibility to spouses and minor children is not even mentioned. But the main line of his insistence is undebatable. Just as God's love is unlimited, so our love must refuse to be fenced in by the limits of human solidarity.

Love without limits

We just touched on the reason why love must be unlimited. Jesus summarizes his demands on us as "Be perfect . . . as your heavenly Father is perfect" (Matthew 5:48). *Perfect* here does not mean irreproachable, flawless, or immune to criticism. It means complete and unlimited. Our love should be unlimited because God's is.

This kind of perfection is what our nonconformity should mean. Anyone can like to hear the children sing, "Red and yellow, black and white, all are precious in his sight," and to give for missions in Africa. But when the question is how to treat those of other ethnicities, social classes, or immigration status, it is not always clear that our love is "perfect." Our limited love is evident in how we as individuals show prejudice and preference in our relations with non-Christians and in how our churches remain skittish about openly fellowshipping with today's equivalents to "Jew and Greek, barbarian and Scythian" (Colossians 3:11).

This unlimitedness of God's love is the real foundation of what we call nonresistance. It is not a rule against killing, nor a failure to see that one government is more just than another, but a simple, humble attempt to love as God does, without "respect of persons" and without discrimination. It is not a special rule about loving our enemies. The enemy is no exception to the general rule about loving everyone. Any refusal to make war that does not involve forsaking all racial prejudice or national hatred, and any charitable giving that does not personally love those helped, is far from what God asks of us. Such action, good as far as it goes, is more like the "righteousness of the scribes and Pharisees," which we must exceed if we are of God's kingdom (Matthew 5:20).

Jesus' love was not only perfect in that it overflowed family limits (Matthew 12:46-50); it was even more remarkably so in its refusal to be guided by ideas of merit. The Father "makes his sun rise on the evil and on the good, and sends rain on the righteous and on the unrighteous" (Matthew 5:45). This is what is shocking about Christian love. It seems more interested in loving than in establishing justice, even to the point of accepting unjust suffering.

The gift of love

Serious and responsible people thought that Jesus was irresponsible with his love. Like the Father, he forgave instead of condemning. He came to seek the lost, not the self-sufficient. This was what the elder son in the parable thought of his father when he welcomed home the worthless younger brother (Luke 15:11-32). It was what the workers who had been in the vineyard all day thought of the master when he gave the latecomers the same wage (Matthew 20:1-16). And so it will always seem to those in whose minds justice comes before love, punishment before forgiveness, merit before grace, and protection before reconciliation.

Such ways of thinking, which refuse to think as God thinks, are not only found in the Pharisaism of the New Testament. We have in ourselves a tendency toward the same reaction. In fact, some of its worst cases throughout history have been in very pious circles—circles where the understanding of God's aggressive, redemptive, all-trusting, all-suffering, all-hoping love has somehow been dimmed by ideas of self-righteousness.

It is normal, in the world where Christian love is not the rule, for another attitude to apply. It is not by accident that parallels to the "Golden Rule" in many other religions are framed negatively: do not to others what you would not want them to do to you. It is normal in public welfare work, for example, to help those who show some signs of gratitude and promise of improvement. It is normal to think that if American food is distributed in foreign countries, the beneficiaries should be grateful and should be friends of the American government. It is normal to say that "charity begins at home" and to be more concerned about a hungry family in the neighborhood than about a starving nation farther away. It is normal to be polite only in polite society, to refrain from shoving only if everyone else awaits his turn in line, to lend only when interest and principal are secured, to "do good to those who do good to you" and "lend to those from whom you hope to receive." This is all normal in the non-Christian world.

But in the sphere of redemption, where the only guide is the always-running-over love of God, such behavior is not normal at all. It is normal to expect us to go the second mile and to "do good, and lend, expecting nothing in return" (Luke 6:35). In our own thinking we must constantly remember to "expect nothing in return." We should ask whether in our relief work we do not expect gratitude or even congratulation, whether in our overseas help we do not expect appreciation or even obedience to our advice, whether in our evangelization we do not expect our own congregations to be strengthened, whether in our giving our right hand is well informed of the doings of the left, whether in our conscientious objection there is uneasiness about the possibility of having an unjustly privileged position instead of giving a suffering witness.

What then is the point of it all? Why should we pour our wealth, time, efforts, and personnel down the infinite drain of the world's neediness if there is no promise of return? Why expend ourselves in helping the ungrateful, forgiving the unrepentant, and witnessing to the hard of heart when we already have enough difficulty being honest and honorable ourselves?

The only answer is that God is that way. God has been pouring love down the drain of our ingratitude for a mighty long time. And the Lord has promised to keep it up as long as the world stands, until the whole story comes to an end. The only reason for our being different from the world, for going out of our way to be loving (how often do we really?) is that God is that way, and we are supposed to resemble God. "Your reward will be great, and you will be *children of the Most High*; for he is kind to the ungrateful and the wicked" (Luke 6:35). "See what love the Father has given us, that we should be called children of God; and that is what we are" (1 John 3:1).

13

The Christian Declaration of Dependence[1]

"All men are endowed by their Creator with certain inalienable rights," according to the Declaration of Independence. Among these rights is liberty. The American and French revolutions, whose anniversaries both fall in July, made "freedom" their rallying cry. By "freedom" they meant the end of submission to a king, taxes that they deemed unfair, and control of thought and expression. They understood freedom as liberation *from* outside influence. They believed that if outside hindrances could be removed, their freedom could be achieved.

One of the major gear shifts involved in learning to think like Christians involves recovering from this revolutionary idea of freedom. The notion of being left alone to do as one

---

1. This chapter was originally published as "The Christian Declaration of Independence," *Christian Living* (July 1955): 27. We have changed the end of the title from "Independence" to "Dependence" based on Yoder's idea for a Christian "declaration of dependence" at the end of the chapter. More than likely, the editors of *Christian Living* titled the original article, since it is standard practice in periodical and book publishing that editors, not authors, have control of titles. Thus, we think the new title better reflects Yoder's own idea.

wants, "free" of any outside influences or controls, is not Christian. Christian freedom is not freedom *from* something as much as freedom *to* and *for* something.

The unfreedom of sin

The Bible is more realistic than the revolutionaries of 1776 (America) or 1789 (France). It tells us that our choice is not between freedom and unfreedom, but between two kinds of slavery. We cannot be our own masters. Being one's own master is the worst form of unfreedom because then one has the most demanding of masters and the least submissive of servants. Still, God gives us the freedom to choose whom we will serve.

It is the feeling of many, especially young people, that freedom means having no rules to follow, no one to give account to, and no one whose wishes have to be considered. In short, it means "being one's own boss." But the Bible tells us that if we do not obey God, we have no choice but to obey sin, which is not freedom at all.

Already in the story of Adam and Eve we see this fatal mistake. They were led to believe that if they really wanted to be free, they would have to disobey God. It was too late before they learned that they were actually making themselves slaves of sin and losing their freedom to live in fellowship with God. They had confused freedom *from* with freedom *to*, and freedom from God which, again, is not freedom at all.

Christian dependence

This is where we must start to understand what the Bible means by redemption. *To redeem* means to ransom or buy back. When the Bible says we needed redemption it means more than our need for forgiveness. It means we were sold into slavery under the power of sin and that we were not free to know and to do the good. We ourselves had absolutely no means of procuring our release. Only a divine intervention could help. The Bible teaches that by becoming an obedient slave, obedient to the point of death, Christ obtained our liberation. He gave his life as a ransom for many. He did so not to make of us free persons, but to make us slaves of God.

The apostle Paul makes this point when he says, "You are not your own. For you were bought with a price; therefore glorify God in your body" (1 Corinthians 6:19-20). In his letter to the Roman churches he emphasizes this again: "Do you not know that . . . you are slaves of the one whom you obey, either of sin, which leads to death, or of obedience, which leads to righteousness? But thanks be to God that you, having once been slaves of sin, have become obedient from the heart . . . and that you, having been set free from sin, have become slaves of righteousness" (Romans 6:16-18).

All our thinking about Christian life is wrong if it does not start from here. What should we think about our bodily appetites and drives? We should not ask whether we have a right to do this or whether we are free to do that. We should begin with "You are not your own" and then search, with God's promised help and that of other Christians, to know what it means to glorify God in our bodies.

What should we think about the liberties we have in free countries where we can "get away with" many kinds of behavior? "As servants of God, live as free people, yet do not use your freedom as a pretext for evil" (1 Peter 2:16). What should young people do with all the freed time and money that they typically have during their teens and early twenties? "So speak and so act as those who are to be judged by the law of liberty" (James 2:12). What shall wage earners or entrepreneurs do with the great freedom they have to spend the fruit of their labor as they wish? What shall Christians do who have been given freedom by their congregations to spend their money as they wish? "For you were called to freedom, brothers and sisters; only do not use your freedom as an opportunity for self-indulgence, but through love become slaves to one another. For the whole law is summed up in a single commandment, 'You shall love your neighbor as yourself'" (Galatians 5:13-14).

Old Testament laws made provision for slaves who preferred remaining in their master's service even when they had the right to be freed (Deuteronomy 15:16). This choice was sealed by a physical mark, a hole pierced in the ear lobe. It very well may be this kind of thing that the apostle Paul is referring to when he writes to the Galatian Christians, "Let no one make trouble for me; for I carry the marks of Jesus branded on my body" (Galatians 6:17). The marks on his body, the scars from the lashings and stonings, which he received as a slave of Christ, were the signs of his belonging to the Lord Jesus as he freely fulfilled what James called "the perfect law, the law of liberty" (James 1:25).

So the Christian declaration of liberty, the starting point of his or her history, is a declaration of dependence. Having learned that everyone who commits sin is a slave to sin, and that "if the Son makes you free, you will be free indeed" (John 8:36), Christians make the free choice of slavery to God. They open their lives to their owner's orders and find the joy of being free for what life was really meant to be. "Where the Spirit of the Lord is, there is freedom. And all of us, with unveiled faces, seeing the glory of the Lord . . . are being transformed into the same image" (2 Corinthians 3:17-18). This is what the New Testament means by saying that we are children of God. This is true liberty, the purpose of God with all creation, the reason humanity has free will. It is the "freedom of the glory of the children of God" (Romans 8:21).

14

The "Greater Righteousness"[1]

We are really not surprised when we read that Jesus expects his followers to be different from pagans. We may be a bit startled to learn how many things in our lives Jesus considers as pagan—like our care for tomorrow or our love for those who love us—but it still seems normal for him to criticize the behavior of heathens.

It is quite another thing when we discover that Jesus cared less for the religious people of his time than he did for the heathen. As his ministry progressed, he taught more and more clearly that his kingdom was not for the pious and self-righteous, but for the sinners and the heathen who repent. Yet this is a teaching that we see in his experience and his earliest discourses (Matthew 5; Luke 4). From the beginnings of his ministry, as reported by the Gospels, Jesus recognized that among those who would have no room for him would be many members of the chosen people. Faithful, even zealous, followers of divinely revealed religion would reject him. To understand what it means for the Christian to be different from the world, we must also take into account the religious world, for the religious kind of conformity is one of the most dangerous.

---

1. "The 'Greater Righteousness,'" *Christian Living* (September 1955): 28–29.

The religious conformity of Jesus' time

The most faithful group of Jews in the time of Jesus was the one called "Pharisees." Their name means "separate." It communicates in a nutshell how they understood faithfulness. Separateness meant avoiding impurity of any kind, keeping all the rules most scrupulously, and expressing their righteousness in every aspect of life, even the smallest matters of diet and clothing. Toward this end they had the help of a body of scholars known as the scribes or the "lettered" who found and interpreted in Scripture the rule to fit every occasion. When the New Testament wants to emphasize a person's conscientiousness and zeal in keeping the law, the best word it can find is "Pharisee" (John 3:1; Philippians 3:5).

In spite of this earnest concern for purity and obedience, something was out of order. This was so much so that the Pharisees receive more of Jesus' hard words than any other group. Somehow all their effort toward nonconformity and keeping the rules did not help them understand or follow Christ. It actually got in their way. So in Matthew's report of Jesus' teaching on his kingdom, we find near the beginning the warning, "unless your righteousness exceeds that of the scribes and Pharisees, you will never enter the kingdom of heaven" (Matthew 5:20).

Nonconformity and rules

To see more of what Jesus meant by such a clear warning, we must look deeper into this insufficient "righteousness." First of all, it was a righteousness of avoidance. There were more rules about what not to do than about what should be done. Most of the encounters we find between Pharisees and Jesus deal with negative rules. Is it permitted to pay taxes to Caesar? Is it lawful to heal on the Sabbath? Why do your disciples transgress the traditions of the elders? Jesus answered by turning from what is forbidden to what is commanded, from the negative to the positive, from what should not be done to what the Pharisees were leaving undone. He turned "Thou shalt not kill" into a command to seek reconciliation, "Thou shalt not swear falsely" into a command to tell the truth, regulations about ritual washings into a reminder that a pure heart is needed. The apostle Paul was following the same procedure when he discarded all the Pharisees' rules by turning the proclamation, "All things are lawful," into the far more demanding principle, "not all things are beneficial" (1 Corinthians 10:23).

The temptation toward an attitude like the Pharisees' is especially great among the more respectable people. In most cases, being respectable means not doing certain things. A child's education begins by learning what not to do: do not play with matches; do not get your feet wet; do not suck your thumb; don't put your feet on the furniture; don't lie, call people names, or steal. A little later they are warned against some kinds of reading matter, some kinds of amusements, and some kinds of thoughts. Usually the fact that "decent people don't" will be sufficient reason for not saying, doing, or thinking certain things. But such rules never quite answer the question, "Why not?" What was necessary to keep children from sucking their thumbs is no longer enough when adolescents are interested in destructive forms of entertainment, when they are called up for military service, or when they are invited into a promising field of employment. This is where the "Thou shalt nots" of tradition break down. There will always be ways of arguing that there is no harm or no sin in certain forms of amusement, in certain forms of military service, or in certain fields of work. It will always be a losing battle to argue that this or that act, way of dressing, or way of spending Sunday is in itself wrong. When nonconformity is stated in such terms, it is pharisaical; not Christian.

But if our nonconformity is not pharisaical, what will it be? Will we have no choice but to do what everyone else does? That is what we must not do. Our choice must be to guide every choice by what Christ did and by what he would do in our place. In fact, Christ *is* in our place. That is what it means to believe in the Holy Spirit. The Holy Spirit is the means by which Christ lives in us. With Christ living in us, how will we act? Like the world? Certainly not! Like the Pharisees? Quite often, yes.

This is the paradox of Christian freedom: that when we give up living by rules and begin living in daily fellowship with Christ, we discover that the rules are helpful after all. We discover that the rules were really meant all the time to help us live in fellowship with Christ. This is what Jesus meant when he said he had come to fulfill the law, not to abolish it. It is what he meant when he told even the Pharisees that their error was not in keeping their rules, but in leaving more important things undone. So even though keeping rules and following a tradition are not the basis of Christian life, followers of Christ will respect any guide that can be a help toward living according to his will and example. Christians will never let themselves think that they are in fellowship with God because they are different from the world, but they will be different from the world because of their fellowship with God.

Nonconformity and humility

A second error of the Pharisees was that their nonconformity, because it was expressed in rules that could easily be kept, was a nonconformity of self-righteousness. They achieved by their own efforts all that God asked of them; so they had the right to be proud of themselves. This was the mistake of the Pharisee in the parable of the Pharisee and the tax collector (Luke 18:9-14). The Pharisee's mistake was not that he kept the rules. Jesus approved of fasting and tithing. The Pharisee's error is that he was proud of himself for keeping rules that were easy to keep. Had he set his standards higher, asking of himself the unselfishness and love that God asked for even in the Old Testament, he would never have forgotten that he needed forgiveness. Just like the tax collector, the Pharisee needed God's help to achieve, even in a slight way, what was truly expected of him.

For those of us who have the New Testament, which tells us more clearly what God expects and reminds us that we can only do it with God, every excuse for a misunderstanding like that of the Pharisees is gone. If our nonconformity is biblical, it will always recognize that we have not accomplished all our duty and that what we have accomplished is, at best, only our duty. Never have we anything to be proud of—not our giving for relief, nor our migration to find freedom of conscience, nor our stable family life, nor our well-run farms. We may only take pride in God's goodness. Before the Sermon on the Mount, it was possible to place the requirements so low that with little effort they could be reached. But the righteousness that Jesus asks for the kingdom is different. The scribes and

Pharisees had gone as far as human righteousness would take them, and it wasn't enough. It falls short of what only God's righteousness, working in and for God's children, can reach.

Nonconformity and evangelism

The Pharisees' third mistake was the one Jesus responded to in the parables of Luke 15 (the prodigal son) and Matthew 20 (the vineyard laborers). Whereas the father's purpose is to save the lost, the elder brother who stayed home and worked, like the workers who toiled in the vineyard all day, thought it unfair of the father to forgive and welcome home the prodigal son. The father's reproach was not that the elder son had stayed home, but that he failed to share in the father's joy when the lost son returned. Such was the attitude of the Pharisees. Their respect for their own respectability was so great that they strove to honor God by keeping God to themselves. Jesus seemed to be quite out of order in associating with the poor and the unclean, with tax collectors and women of ill fame. Their error was forgetting that God's promise to Abraham, of which they were so proud, was meant to be a blessing to all peoples. Those who understand God's goodness can never keep it for themselves. So Jesus concluded that the Pharisees had their minds closed even to the Old Testament's truth. They had ears that could not hear and eyes that could not see that they were closing their own way to repentance (Matthew 13:13-15).

Nor was the Christian church free of this attitude, even at the very beginning. There was a strong faction in the Jerusalem church, if not a wider majority, that resisted every time the Holy Spirit attempted to carry the message to non-Israelites without first requiring them to be good Jews. This group even bore the name Pharisees (Acts 15:5). Throughout at least the first forty years of the church's life, they attempted to hinder mission work, especially that of the apostle Paul, in order to keep the gospel for themselves. But the gospel kept for oneself is no gospel.

Christian nonconformity may be distinguished from pharisaical nonconformity right at this point. Christian nonconformity is an aid to evangelism, a platform, so to speak, from which God's invitation to fellowship may be proclaimed more clearly and so that the invitation and the decision it requires may be understood. Evangelism without nonconformity is not quite honest. It broadcasts the invitation without defining the commitment God wants. Sub-Christian nonconformity is a barrier to evangelism because it asks more than God does, tries to keep God to itself, and forgets that if there is no invitation to fellowship there is really no church. The church is not a society of righteous people. It is the bearer of the message that God was in Christ, reconciling the world to God's own self. This message makes the church different from the world. The church believes it, lives it, and proclaims it. This makes the church a misfit in the world just like its Master, who lived and proclaimed the same message. Its life, nonconformity, and "greater righteousness" are nothing but the church's living fellowship with God.

15

The Christian's Peace of Mind[1]

Ours is an age of return to religion. Publishers, politicians, journalists, the entertainment industry, and the military are all affected. On all sides it is becoming respectable to show a new interest in "faith," "moral values," and "peace of mind." Church and synagogue enjoy growing respect as bulwarks of what makes life worthwhile and safeguards of the nation's inner strength.

It would come as a surprise to many who encourage and profit from this "return to religion" to discover what the Christian attitude toward religion is. The founders of Christianity—Christ, the apostles, and the prophets before them—made it clear that they had no great respect for religion as such. They identified it as a manifestation of what is wrong with humanity. Those seeking to distinguish between the Christian and the world would therefore do well to investigate the difference between Christianity and religion.

Religion's peace of mind and Christianity's burning unrest

Christianity itself is a religion, we are told. True enough. Seen from the outside, the Christian faith has much in common

---

1. "The Christian's Peace of Mind," *Christian Living* (November 1955): 32–33, 38.

with other ways of relating oneself to the world of values. We may admit without hesitation that such comparisons can be made. Yet what matters about Christianity is the way in which it differs from, not the way it resembles, other religions. That in some ways Gandhi or Confucius taught or behaved like Christ is interesting, but how Christ differs from them is what saves us.

One of the Christian reactions to religion is pity. In it we may observe human emptiness and our need for truth. It was in such a tone that Paul began one of his sermons. He observed that the Athenians to whom he spoke were very religious people (Acts 17:22). He recognized in their religiosity a symptom of their hunger for truth that they could not find by themselves.

Religion was considered an essential part of civilization. The gods were thought to dispense good or ill fortune, and their favor was the only assurance of success, happiness, and social unity. In our day the same is the case. "Religion" is a safeguard of the "American way of life." Membership in a good church is one way to climb the social ladder, and the best-selling books are ones that offer "peace of mind." Religion is a source of calm, a protection against maladjustment, a proof that the universe and humankind are friendly. Above all, it is nothing disturbing or unseemly.

That shows us why it was such a blow to the respectable religious people of Athens to hear that things were not really that way at all. Paul told them that instead of reassurance there was a warning of judgment. He proclaimed that instead of calm there was a tremendous urgency of decision. The hearers were divided into believers and unbelievers. They were not united in the cultural advance of which Athens was proud.

For the Athenians, religion was a matter of decoration, not truth. Many cults got along well together because none of them made any exclusive claims. A person could support several different temples in order to be as well insured as possible. Yet Paul spoke of a God who claimed to be unique, final, and tolerating no competition. He proclaimed a God whose will is made known in one unrepeatable man, Jesus. Today's religion is no different. A rabbi or a Catholic priest can write just as good a book about peace of mind as a Protestant pastor can. Politicians who avoid defining too clearly what they mean by an appeal to "our heritage of faith" will gain better support for their immigration restrictions, protective tariffs, and military strategies than those who raise the question of right and wrong.

Even churches are wary of the question of truth. Their colleges have courses in "religion" where the problem of evil or the theoretical possibility of immortality are discussed with great learnedness, but where Christ's demand for total decision would not quite be in place. The churches cooperate to "church" a new housing development. *To church* is a verb meaning to supply an area with a religious edifice and a professional pastor. What such pastors believe or what theological point of view they represent is of little importance, since their main activity will be counseling, organizing parties, performing marriages, and assuring people that all is well.

The Christian message cuts across all of these trends in our day as in Paul's. Since it begins with a total claim to truth, it tolerates no theorizing about the problem of evil or immortality. Since truth demands personal decision, it brings not social unity but a new kind of disunity. There are those who are open to its revolution and those who prefer that life go on as usual. Jesus warned his listeners that he came not to bring peace but a sword—to provoke a decision that would result in disunity (Matthew 10:34). In place of peace of mind and adjustment to things as they are, he kindled a burning unrest in the hearts of his disciples that would not be quenched until their lives were fully spent in a constant maladjustment to things as they are. They would remain unsatisfied until they proclaimed God's judgment on the world and scattered the leaven of God's reconstruction of things as they should be.

Every time the New Testament wants to clarify its fundamental message, it tells us in strong terms not that we should adapt ourselves to life as it is, but that things must change utterly. It tells us not that we need to be "churched," counseled, and soothed, but that we need to be completely made over according to a new pattern. That pattern is a human being who was so different that even his closest friends could not quite understand him. His insistence on the question of truth was so bothersome that the religious people had him put to death. Sometimes Scripture states this in terms of being born from above (John 3:3), sometimes of dying and being resurrected (Colossians 2:12), sometimes of undressing and putting on a new person (Ephesians 4:24). Always it is clear that Christian life must be different from a calmer and better adjusted return to life as we lived it before.

That difference is what we call nonconformity. It means we have no room for any kind of "religion" that undertakes less than the complete remodeling of our lives. We should beware of any assurances that we are basically all right. We should be suspicious of the claim that only a little more sociability, relaxation, meditation, tolerance, and effort to understand our neighbors will make the world one big happy family with everyone content to live according to their own convictions and let the others do the same.

When religion has nothing to do with shaking up our lives, it has to find some other excuse for taking our time. We must find any number of things to do which may be tried as substitutes. It is possible, for instance, to enhance the beauty of the Sunday morning service with music, symbolism, liturgy, and an artfully composed sermon. It is possible to advocate "faith" as a support for one's patriotism, as evidenced by the printing of "In God We Trust" on US postage stamps or the inclusion of the phrase "under God" in the Pledge of Allegiance. It is possible to elevate to a central position hard work or community betterment. Any of these values becomes idolatry when they are made primary. It thus becomes even clearer that religion is desired for its decorative effect, group unity, or a quaint reminder of bygone ways. It can provide ceremonial frill on the fringes of life, but it may not supply truth, commands, judgments, or permanent dissatisfaction with oneself and the world.

To be Christian means to have found in Jesus Christ so clear and so imperative a revelation of truth that there remains no way to feel at home in the world or satisfied with oneself. Yet at the same time the inner harmony of will—which our contemporaries and the Athenians seek without finding it in all their reassuring religions—is granted only to those who have undergone this process of dying to themselves and receiving a new life in Christ. The person who seeks peace, calm, and stability will not find them. The person who seeks first God's kingdom finds that the rest is a by-product: "righteousness and peace and joy in the Holy Spirit" (Romans 14:17). Whoever saves their life will lose it. Whoever seeks for themselves consolation, reassurance, and stability will finally close themselves in with their own self-centeredness. Only those who lose their life and abandon all interest in feeling their own psychic pulse will one day be startled to find that their maladjustments and fears are being transformed in the victory that overcomes the world.

Nonconformity is not faithfulness to ancestors but to God

If the Greeks made of religion a search for novelty and self-fulfillment, there were others who understood religion in a quite different way. They had the privilege of knowing the true God. That God had spoken to their fathers and they continued to be proud of what God said. Theirs was religion of tradition and conscientious obedience in the smallest details. Their entire life was dedicated to the pursuit of righteousness in the best way they knew. For these people, the custodians of divine revelation and the zealous seekers after righteousness, Jesus had many a hard word. Paul was not the first to criticize inadequate religion. Jesus had begun by proclaiming the insufficiency of the religion of the most faithful Jews. "Unless your righteousness exceeds that of the scribes and Pharisees," he told his disciples, "you will never enter the kingdom of heaven" (Matthew 5:20).

It is no surprise that such an attitude eventually drove the very religious scribes and Pharisees to seek a way of getting rid of Jesus. For in condemning their Sabbath observance, their ways of tithing, of fasting, of praying, and even their claims to be descendants of Abraham, he undermined all that they held sacred. They expected the coming Messiah to shake up the Gentiles. They hadn't thought it would apply to them. But Jesus uncovered that in their search for righteousness they had placed the form before the content and that their piety had ceased to serve God's loving work in the world.

We too, who would like to count ourselves among the righteous, may do well to ask whether we do not sometimes strain out gnats and swallow camels (Matthew 23:24), whether our forms of simple life do not cover a special kind of luxury,

whether what we call separation from the world is not sometimes a form of disinterestedness in the fate of our neighbor,
whether the carefulness of our nonconformity does not get in
the way of our higher righteousness, whether in our earnestness to "do this" we are not "neglecting the others" (Matthew
23:23). God does not ask of us the faithfulness of our ancestors. He asks for the openness to be led as they were into the
higher righteousness of life in the Spirit of God and the fellowship of the church. The more our piety and our principles
approach what God wants of us, the greater is the danger that
we make them substitutes for constant fellowship with God.

The idea of faithfulness to the "God of our ancestors"
gave the Pharisees a comfortable feeling, much more comfortable than having God on hand here and now. With their
set of rules for every situation they could have an answer,
always be in good standing, always have God on their side.
But having Jesus around was different. He caught them up
on points that their rules didn't cover. He showed them that
the rules were not being made to fit people's needs as God
had meant them to. Even if at one time those rules had been
received by divine revelation, they had to step back when
God came into the world to bring them up to date.

The Holy Spirit guides our nonconformity

And now we have the promise, or the warning, that God
will keep breaking into our situation to awaken us to new
problems and lead us to new answers that will faithfully
express the truth once and for all given to humanity in God's
Son. "I still have many things to say to you," Jesus said, "but
you cannot bear them now. When the Spirit of truth comes,
he will guide you into all the truth; for he will not speak on
his own . . . he will take what is mine and declare it to you"
(John 16:12-14).

The living presence of Christ in his Spirit holds the old and
new answers together, correcting both the Athenians who
are indifferent to the truth and the Pharisees who think they
have it under control. That is why Christian faith is more
than a religion. It is a Person whose presence and power are
realities, not just symbols for states of mind. Jesus promised,
"I will ask the Father, and he will give you another Advocate,

to be with you forever. This is *the Spirit of truth, whom the world cannot receive*, because it neither sees him nor knows him. You know him, because he abides in you, and he will be in you" (John 14:16-17). That is our nonconformity.

16

Love Seeks Not Its Own[1]

"You were taught to put away your former way of life
. . . and to be renewed in the spirit of your minds, and
to clothe yourselves with the new self, created according to the likeness of God in true righteousness and
holiness. . . . Thieves must give up stealing; rather let
them labor and work honestly with their own hands,
so as to have something to share with the needy."
(Ephesians 4:22-24, 28)

The Bible has a surprising way of turning commandments
inside out. Jesus turned "Thou shalt not kill" into an order
to seek reconciliation and the warning against breaking an
oath into a condemnation of all swearing. Here the apostle
Paul gives a new positive meaning to "Thou shalt not steal."
After having described the change which makes a Christian
different from the world, he tells us that the alternative to
theft is honest labor.

What is wrong with theft is not, first of all, that it is an
offense against the institution of private property. In that case
the alternative to theft would have been leaving other people's
things alone. Paul condemns stealing because those who steal

---

1. Originally published as "Love Seeketh Not Its Own," *Christian
Living* (January 1956): 26–28.

are not working. Such persons receive their livelihood without making a contribution to the economy. Their efforts subtract from rather than add to the total well-being of society.

Already we see how different the Christian viewpoint is from the world. The ordinary way of looking at things begins with personal rights of ownership. Theft is understood as an offense only against the personal interest of an owner. If no owner is offended (as in gambling or speculation) there is no theft. An individual under this system will work only if he can expect reward in the form of personal property or wages. Such a person will lend or give property only in the hope of receiving interest in return. Economists study the relationship between the various individuals who make up a society, all of whose actions are assumed to be governed by the search for more personal property (the "profit motive"). This is the attitude Jesus identified as normal for "sinners." Such people return good for good and lend at interest.

The law of giving

The Christian line of thinking is different because it cannot begin with the idea of personal ownership. "You are not your own" is the starting point for thinking about property, work, and every other aspect of nonconformity. The apostle Paul does not often use the word *stewardship*, but all that the word signifies is involved when he says, "you were bought with a price; therefore glorify God in your body" (1 Corinthians 6:20).

From this beginning it is a short step to the awareness that, if the Christian belongs to God, then the law of that person's life must be giving, as Christ gave himself for humanity. Then it is normal to work and to give without expecting recompense. Jesus tells us that, just as God is good to the ungrateful and the selfish, so the Christian should "do good, and lend, expecting nothing in return," so that "you will be children of the Most High" (Luke 6:35). Our motive for giving generously is that we may resemble the heavenly Father.

This leads to a much more profound understanding of theft. If giving is the law of one's life, Christians are really stealing from their neighbors every time they fail to serve and every time they fail to work and to give freely and without seeking recompense.

It is clear then why the Christian will not gamble or seek income through speculation or charging interest. Such practices render no service to one's neighbor; therefore the income they bring is unjust, even though it may often be hard to determine who really suffers from them. If our morals consisted of not hurting anyone, then certain kinds of speculation and market manipulation might be permissible. But when our command is to serve, there is no more room for sources of income that do not result from service.

The first Mennonites were for this reason very critical of the merchant's profession. They judged that the margin between the sale and purchase price of merchandise was a kind of speculation out of proportion to the services rendered. Even more insistently, they refused to believe that a Christian can charge interest, leaning for support on the clear words of Christ in Luke 6:35, where the command not to expect any return on loans comes in the same breath with "love your enemies."

Yet these early Mennonites did not upset the existing social order. They were willing to pay interest where it was demanded, just as they paid taxes. They simply denied that a Christian could justify making a profit on giving when giving should be done for its own sake out of love. They did not deny that the profit motive was necessary in the world, but among the people of God charging interest was forbidden, equivalent to theft. We must admit that they seem to have had Jesus on their side.

It may well be argued that contemporary rates of interest on investments and the modern merchant's profit margin have nothing to do with the abusive interest rates and speculative prices of the Middle Ages, nor with the interest rates of Bible times. It may be that assuming the risk of investment is itself a service to society that is worthy of recompense. It may also be that even furnishing funds is already such a service and that the merchant performs services of warehousing and distribution that deserve reward. Well and good. It is not the purpose of this article to deal with such arguments. The fact remains that, even if they are true, they do not release the Christian from nonconformity to the world in the economic sphere.

Christian critique of communism and capitalism

This means a critical eye toward all of one's economic life in light of the rule that working and giving are normal for the Christian. Since a major element of the world's tension grows out of a clash between two economic orders, we must strive to understand the Christian's viewpoint concerning that clash.

Americans usually begin by criticizing communism. This is an easy exercise because it is always simpler to criticize those who are absent than to correct one's own errors. The path of nonconformity will be to refuse all black-and-white judgments and all taking sides in a worldly struggle. We must strive to see both sides as God sees them.

Communism is, of course, open to criticism, in varying ways, depending on whether one designates by that word an economic system, a philosophy, a religion, or a political system. Yet in full awareness of these criticisms, and in spiritual fellowship with those who suffered for their faith under communist governments, the Christian who lives in an anticommunist world will be more interested in the fact that many such criticisms apply equally to capitalism.

Communism as a philosophy is materialistic. It is built upon the assumption that people act only in line with their economic self-interest. The Christian knows that such a philosophy, which denies God's lordship over history and human freedom to obey God, is false. Yet Christians will not forget that capitalism is built on the same foundation when it assumes that making profit is the only motive behind human endeavors. It can happen, of course, that an individual capitalist can be better than the capitalistic system and can act for other motives than profit. In such a case that person is no longer acting as a consistent capitalist. Communists can also be better than their system. If we judge the system on the basis of individuals, we are no longer judging the system. Both systems are at the base materialistic.

The governments of the Soviet Union, of China, and of their satellite states, which inaccurately call themselves communist, are built to a great degree upon police coercion and the denial of individual liberties. In their foreign relations, they operate according to the belief that might makes right. Thus they are a menace to international order. This, too, must be condemned by the Christian.

Yet the Christian will not forget that many capitalistic governments—some of them supported directly by North Americans and their allies—also use unjustified policing methods. If one may judge by the importance given to military preparations in comparison to peaceful means of seeking understanding, one can hardly avoid the impression that trust in violence is not a monopoly of communist states. Russia has never exploded an atomic bomb outside its borders, whether in war or peace. The United States has done so repeatedly. The United States has had air bases aimed against Russia on the continents of Europe and Asia. Russia has no air bases in the Americas, nor is there even one in Guatemala.[2]

Such comparisons could go on much longer, but the point is clear. Christians must be clear in our judgment on all human "isms," including communism. In many respects we will prefer, relatively, the American economic and political system to that of Soviet Russia. Yet we will see deeply enough to understand that the faults of communism lie not in the system, but in sinful humanity. We will be careful to see the same faults just as clearly when they show themselves in capitalism. Discussions about the ideal economic system are of minor interest for the Christian. What concerns us is living in love where we are. This means being more aware of worldliness surrounding us than of the sins of an "enemy" on the other side of the globe.

The law of giving does not underwrite capitalism

The Christian living in the Western world will therefore be more interested in a careful judgment about capitalism than in an easy condemnation of communism. This question falls into two parts. Often we meet the argument that, because the Bible recommends giving and forbids theft, it really means to teach us that private property is anchored in the will of God. It therefore follows that capitalism is also God's favorite economic system. Things are really not that simple.

---

2. Guatemala and the Soviet Union had diplomatic relations during the Cold War.

In the Bible, ownership of property is presupposed, but not recommended. Property is part of the world order, like violence, which is accepted as a background for the Bible's teaching, but not advocated. The command to give takes for granted that we have property, but does not say we should keep it. In fact Jesus warns clearly against accumulating property. The command not to steal takes for granted that others will possess property, but does not say that we should. What the Bible takes for granted is not thereby approved. The command to turn the other cheek assumes that someone will strike us. We cannot therefore conclude that striking people is normal and God's will for us. The institution of private property, like its opposite in communism, is a human attempt to deal with the problem of ownership in a practical way. Private property is not a divine ordinance. If private property is preferable for the non-Christian world, under certain restraints, this is due to practical reasons, not divine commands.

Yet the defense of private property does not suffice to justify capitalism. There is private property under socialism as well, and in most kinds of communism where the individual owns their own food and clothing. Nor is it capitalism in the exact sense of the word when a farmer owns his farm, an artisan his tools, or a rural mail carrier his car. Capitalism really begins only when individuals keep more of their wealth than they need to feed, clothe, house, and educate their family and possess the tools of the trade, and when somebody invests the additional wealth, at interest, in the tools of someone else's trade. Neither of these aspects, keeping more wealth than one needs and owning someone else's means of subsistence, is authorized in the New Testament.

Free enterprise falls short of God's will

The Christian's interest is not whether one economic system or another is justified. The real problem is how to be separate from the world in the midst of whatever system surrounds us. For North Americans, this means separation from those aspects of the "free enterprise" or "profit motive" system that fall short of God's will. Some of them may be worth naming.

1. Up to the limits of one's income, individuals fix their own standard of living. They decide what they need to feed, clothe, and house themselves, and how much will be left for other uses. This leads to great differences in standards, often with little relation to merit or need. On the Christian level, this means that everyone is finally their own master in how seriously they take stewardship.
2. The multiplicity of free producers, buyers, and sellers leads to overlapping and competing efforts. This leads to the waste of advertising and the theft of speculation, and thereby to economic inefficiency and loss. It is not certain that another economic system would be more efficient for the world, but among Christians it should be possible to take such waste seriously and work against it.
3. The ownership of other people's means of subsistence—that is, ownership through invested capital of the tools with which others work—can lead to unjust treatment of those workers. This is less the case in North America today than at other times and places. For this reason, North Americans cannot understand why capitalism is disliked in the rest of the world without using their imaginations. The fact remains that places where there is enough for everyone, including the workers, are the exception and not the rule.
4. The search for profit through monopoly or influence on government can lead to restraints on free enterprise that contribute to the detriment of one part of society. For example, certain North American industries protect their favored positions through tariff walls.
5. The "everyone for themselves" attitude of the world has led Christians to feel that each individual must accumulate on a private basis a financial reserve against old age or unexpected needs. The commercial insurance business provides an equivalent to such savings that is less costly in the short view and more costly in the end. In either form this search for security is costly for the individual and for society, and actually quite insecure.

6. The system tends to seek its own preservation, even at the cost of war.
7. The tendency is to invest where the probable interest rate or security is the greatest, not where the investment is most useful to society.

Christian giving as nonconformity to capitalism

With respect to all these aspects of the economic system which surrounds us, Christians should pursue loving acts and attitudes that will set them apart from the world. This is not for the sake of being set apart, but because of their love for the world and the needy. Here are seven examples of what that should look like.

1. Christians should seek ways, within the Christian fellowship, to express sincerely the biblical teaching that "you are not your own." Through mutual admonition and study they could seek ways of "depersonalizing" their ownership, such as turning their holdings over to foundations or nonprofit corporations. They should also remind themselves to be careful in estimating their "needs," such as budgeting their expenditures on the basis of the average worker's income.
2. Through such means as cooperatives, standardization, and consumer's research, Christians should seek to decrease the waste of duplication and advertising. We should avoid speculation and gambling because, in light of the biblical idea of work, both practices are theft.
3. Through such means as worker ownership, profit sharing, and worker management schemes, Christian owners will seek to guarantee the full dignity of those whom their wealth employs.
4. Christians should condemn economic injustices such as the protective tariff. Insofar as we benefit from such injustice, as is sometimes unavoidable, we should seek the most appropriate way to pass that benefit on to the needy. We should also make known

our own readiness to accept the adjustments that would come from its abolition.

5. The Christian fellowship should obey the numerous biblical commands to support the aged, widows, and orphans. Through congregational and other mutual aid arrangements, its members must dare to take seriously the Bible's warnings against accumulating capital for personal security.

6. The Christian should avoid, with a special vigilance, any temptation to be drawn into a crusade, military or "peaceful," for any economic system. We must remember that neither the preservation nor the reformation of the world is the Christian's first assignment.

7. Christians should avoid "good" investments if the security or the interest rate is based on mistreatment of workers, illegality or speculation, or the production of war materials or luxury goods. Christians should accept greater risks and lower income if they can enable useful production. A Christian should, in fact, be ready to accept no interest and to run the risk of total loss whenever the need demands it (Luke 6:35).

Economic nonconformity is deeper than military opposition

A study of Christian history demonstrates that nonconformity can degenerate in two ways. It can take the form of stubborn insistence on a peculiarity which has lost all moral meaning, such as matters of language or culture. Or, it can be abandoned when one no longer sees clearly at what point a difference from the world is morally necessary or worthy of suffering. In both cases—the hardening into cultural isolation and the sacrifice of separation—the reason is the same. People forget that their separation from the world is a moral matter, a question of obedience to God. In both cases the result is the same: the salt has lost its savor.

There was a time when Mennonites gave their lives for their convictions about baptism or the oath. Now such issues do not matter enough to anyone to bring about suffering. Not long ago, Christians in North America still suffered, or at least sacrificed, for their convictions about military service. Now, such cases are rare. In general, alternative service possibilities are such that it "pays" to be a conscientious objector if one accepts the draft enough to register and accept alternative service.[3] It may not be out of order to ask whether the deepening of nonconformity that the Lord asks of us today is not in the field of economics.

The Hutterite Brethren, taking as their example the Jerusalem church, feel that every Christian should entirely renounce personal property. This belief may be theoretically an error, but practically it is a powerful truth that such a way of life can lead to great effectiveness in stewardship. The only answer to such a challenge is to consider the example of the New Testament congregations of Antioch, Philippi, and Corinth. This means to take stewardship so seriously, to give and serve so completely and consistently, that it is clear to the entire world that we have forsaken all to follow Jesus. So far, we haven't given the world that impression.

---

3. While peace church objectors to the military were assigned to labor camps called "Civilian Public Service" during World War II—which is the model Yoder is working with in this early essay—today conscientious objectors to war are not sent to labor camps, prison, or assigned to any other alternative service in the United States or Canada. In other countries, such as Germany, where the draft is still in effect, some kind of alternative service is required for those who refuse military service.

17

Rejoicing in Hope[1]

One of the weakest words in the English language is *hope*. When something is certain to happen, so certain that we make our plans accordingly, we may say we expect that event, we count on it, we look forward to it, or we anticipate it. We would not say that we hope for it. To hope, in contemporary usage, involves an element of uncertainty or even unlikelihood. If we hope for something to happen, we are not sure of it, we do not count on it, and we probably do not factor it into our planning. The current meaning of the word *hope* is nearer to desire than to expectation. In fact, "I hope so" is a polite way to say, "probably not."

It is understandable, then, why it is difficult to grasp what the Bible means when it speaks of hope. It has a far different sense. Far from designating a leaning toward optimism and a refusal to look unpleasant facts in the face, hope is one of the strongest expressions in the New Testament. It means the strongest kind of certainty, an expectation so sure that those who do not make their plans accordingly are foolish.

Such a certainty can have only one source. No human promise, plan, or program can warrant risking our lives on the chances that it will be carried out. Only the promise

---

1. "Rejoicing in Hope," *Christian Living* (February 1956): 32–33.

of God can justify hope, in the biblical sense of the word. That is why Paul once described pagans as "having no hope and without God in the world" (Ephesians 2:12). "Without God" and "without hope" are the same thing.

Meaningful life

Pagan philosophers and founders of religions, when attempting to understand the meaning of life and history, generally choose some concept of endless repetition. Such is the case for the materialist who claims that all is a recurring interplay of atoms and Hindus who speak of recurring incarnations. It is true for the Greek philosopher speaking of the "wheel of time" and the primitive persons whose lives are tied to the cycle of the seasons. Pagans do not expect themselves, or world history, to "get anywhere." Families, cities, and nations rise and fall and leave things just as before. There is no "meaning of history." Humanity's only problem is to fit into the rotation of events in the least uncomfortable way.

Only "with God" can time and effort, life and history, have meaning. Only where people know that their lives are in the hand of a purposeful Creator, capable of attaining God's goals, can their lives take on sense in the wider frame of events. Only in light of the promise of a sovereign God can the crisscrossing threads of human life and death, sacrifice and self-affirmation, devotion and defeat, take on pattern and permanence. Even in paganism, those philosophies that believe that human events have timeliness and direction (such as Marxism and rationalist belief in progress) have received the idea from their Jewish-Christian heritage.

Hope is patient and resolute

One helpful way to understand what is different about the Christian will be to study the effect of hope on that person's life. We might ask what this person hopes for; what he or she expects, when they expect it, and how. Such a study would lead us too far afield. Let us rather ask only what it will mean when Christians, in hope, count on the promise of God and "plan accordingly."

The defining characteristic of Christian hope is patience or steadfastness (1 Thessalonians 1:3). The firmness with which we face adversity is the measure of our belief in the final triumph of God. Hope is that quality of confidence that enables living as if God were to have the last word when at present that does not appear to be the case.

There are two ways of rejecting Christian hope. One is to agree with Christians that there will be a last word and that life makes sense, but then to disagree as to what that word will be and who will speak it. Chief of the alternative hopes is the belief that force will win out in the end and that "planning accordingly" will involve accumulating worldly power. From Cain to NATO, the company of those whose hope is that "might will make right" is great. Jesus met this kind of hope in a very popular form. The Zealots of his time, from whose ranks came several of his disciples, meant to restore Israel's freedom to serve God using the means that promised results. That meant violent revolution against the Roman occupation.

When they spoke of the Messiah they meant a political deliverer. The temptation to accept their hope and their weapons always lay before Jesus. His disciples understood him that way when they were shocked by the cross. Pilate, although he knew better, accepted the same view when he executed Jesus as a pretender to the throne and released in his place another Zealot. Yet in the face of universal misunderstanding Jesus chose, and followed steadfastly, the path that led to the cross for the clear reason that he had hope. He knew absolutely that love, not force, will have the last word. He planned accordingly.

Hope and faith

At this point hope coincides with faith. Many who read the beginning verses of Hebrews 11—"faith . . . is the conviction of things not seen"—come to think that faith means saying yes to anything one is told. In their eyes, the strongest faith is able to assent to the most unlikely and impossible doctrines. This leads to the idea that to believe means to accept a doctrine. This, in turn, leads to the notion that to believe in Christ means to accept, with or without proof or explanation, a doctrine about his nature, birth, death, resurrection, or coming. Now it might sometimes be the case that the Christian should believe doctrines without understanding them, but such an idea is not what the book of Hebrews is talking about. The interest in chapter 11 is not in doctrinal faith, but faith that is bound to hope (v. 1)—faith that draws near to God and counts on God rewarding those who seek him (v. 6).

Faith is, in other words, just like hope. It is confidence in the ultimate rightness that enables people to serve God in the face of apparent failure. The entire chapter of Hebrews 11 is a list of heroes. They are not remembered for believing doctrines, but for trusting God enough to obey when it did not seem to be the sensible thing to do. The climax of the series is Christ himself, "who for the sake of the joy that was set before him endured the cross" (Hebrews 12:2), and the call to the believer to "lay aside every weight," to "run with perseverance the race" (v. 1), not to "grow weary or lose heart" (v. 3). Thus the Christian's faith, hope, and nonconformity meet at the point where he or she follows the call to discipleship and accepts the seemingly weak and ineffective tools of love.

Those who hope neither in God nor in any human have only despair left. Despair is also an answer to the question of hope. It says that there is no hope, no meaning to life. All one can do is adjust oneself to events with a minimum of effort and a maximum of comfort. Such an attitude is farther from Christianity than false forms of hope, which at least give life some sort of meaning. Despair need not always designate a state of melancholy. There are people whose lack of real hope and purpose permits them a carefree kind of happiness that Christians cannot share. The scientist who takes measurements without asking about truth; the devotees who make of art, sport, or the automobile ends in themselves; the mothers who look no farther than the day's housework; the fathers who see their work only as a means of livelihood—all may embody forms of hopelessness or aimlessness, despite being occupied and even useful.

Nonconformity, hope, and missions

If, as we have been saying, Christians are different in that they have a purpose, an expectation that dominates life to the point of enabling them to sacrifice and suffer, then we are bound to ask whether they have the right to keep this hope private. If it is for us a certainty, then we will not be able to believe that it is certain only for ourselves. If it were only for a private individual, it would not be certain, but only an illusion. If it is founded in God, then it is as true for our neighbors as for us, and our neighbors should know about it. We can understand that a strong and vibrant Christian hope is closely linked to evangelism and missions. Christ's Great Commission answers a question about hope (Acts 1:6) and it remains in effect until the "end of the age" (Matthew 28:20).

Here we have the ultimate measure of our Christian nonconformity. Nonconformity is grounded in hope, and hope is a message to be proclaimed to the world. True nonconformity is therefore inseparable from proclamation. The difference between the Christian and the world should serve as a podium, not as a fence. If our nonconformity is forbidding instead of inviting, law instead of gospel, calculated instead of creative, then we may well ask whether it is founded in hope or in fear and despair. We should ask whether its trust is in God's power to change people or in a human pattern to keep them from changing. The model for our nonconformity is in the same person as our hope. Since "we will be like him, for we will see him as he is," therefore "all who have this hope in him purify themselves, just as he is pure" (1 John 3:2-3). When our distinctiveness proclaims that hope, it will be a work of God.[2]

---

2. Readers interested in a study of what the Christian hopes for are referred to Paul Erb, *The Alpha and the Omega* (Scottdale, PA: Herald Press, 1955).

Part Three

Conforming to Christ

18

The Meaning of the Cross[1]

There are four sides to my message this morning. One is to speak on today's Sunday school topic, "Jesus Accepts the Cross," with reference to John 18–19. These chapters recount the passion of Jesus from the Garden of Gethsemane to his burial. Second, I was asked to talk about why there needed to be a cross. What does it mean that we need to be saved? This is a deeply theological question. Third, today is when most Christians celebrate Palm Sunday. We remind ourselves of when Jesus came at the head of a nonviolent procession to take over Jerusalem symbolically. That was the beginning of the end of his life. That was when Jerusalem's government resisted him and began the procedures that led to his death. Fourth, this is a day of national mourning because, again in our time, a hostile city took the life of a good man—a man who was preparing to lead a nonviolent march to communicate to the government of that city something about the meaning of righteousness. We would not be a part of today's

---

1. Yoder preached this sermon at Prairie Street Mennonite Church in Elkhart, Indiana, on Palm Sunday, April 5, 1968, the day after Martin Luther King Jr. was assassinated—an event to which Yoder repeatedly refers in the sermon. The audiotape is available at HM6-305 Box 1, Russell Krabill Tapes, Mennonite Church USA Archives, Goshen, Indiana.

world if, as part of our asking about Jesus' cross, we did not ask why this assassination also had to be. We would not be a part of today's world if we went on with business as usual, worship as usual, without also relating Jesus to the events of this week.

Jesus accepts the cross

Why then did it have to happen? Why did Jesus have to accept the cross? Part of the New Testament's answer is that it was for our sins. But what does that mean? What is the connection between our sins and the cross? What does the cross do to our sins? What do our sins do to make the cross necessary?

Another biblical phrase is that it was "according to Scripture." It was foretold. It was known that it had to be this way. But again, that is no real answer to the question, "Why did it have to happen?" Why does Scripture say that this is what happens to the Servant of the Lord?

A further picture we are given is that it was a sacrifice, something like the sacrifices of the Old Testament temple. But why should there be a sacrifice? What does a sacrifice do? The book of Hebrews tells us that the thought of sacrifice had to be changed to fit Jesus. Instead of talking about rituals or something that is done to the body of an animal, we must talk about the perfect obedience of Jesus as a human.

There are many more answers in the Bible to the question about why Jesus had to die. Technically, we call this the doctrine of the atonement.[2] Every civilization to which the church has come, every place and every period in which Christians have lived and tried to make sense of their faith, has had its own view of the meaning of evil, suffering, and death. In every age, Christians have therefore found a way to describe humanity's need and a way to describe how the cross of Jesus speaks to this need.

---

2. In the original document, Yoder notes that the Sunday school curriculum for that day refers to six different biblical explanations of Jesus' death, offered by Mennonite theologian J. C. Wenger, and that there would be more if we went through the history of the Christian church. For Wenger's list see J.C. Wenger, *Introduction to Theology* (Scottdale, PA: Herald Press, 1956), 200–205.

Two traditional answers on the meaning of the cross

In order to sharpen our vision for what seems to be the best answer, let's look at two other answers first.

First, we modern people are trained to think of ourselves as individual personalities. We are very aware of our feelings about things, of our sensitivities, of our honesty, and of our integrity. Parents are taught to be concerned about their children's personalities. Our civilization is full of psychiatry and counseling language. We talk about complexes and problems. We claim each other this way. So we tend to say that the man who shot Martin Luther King Jr. was just sick.

Sometimes we take this kind of attitude to Jesus as well. Every person is selfish and that selfishness expresses itself in hatred and vengefulness. When someone hurts me, I want to hurt someone else. Retaliation doesn't really help us get over it inside. It certainly doesn't change things outside when we respond to evil with evil. But we feel a drive to do it anyway. So what is wrong with the human person is that we are vengeful. We are lost because we are in a vicious circle of vengeance and more vengeance, repaying the hurt we have received by hurting someone else, who also has to lash out in return.

Most of the time the people we lash out against are partly to blame, which allows me to feel righteous in my revenge. I can say that I am taking revenge in the name of law and order, peace in the streets, legitimate self-defense, or to teach the other party a lesson. But what if the other people are blameless? What if they did nothing wrong? What if the thing they did that made me angry was unselfish, was right, or was a good deed? What if my hatefulness against them was entirely my own fault?

Then it just might happen, if I am at all decent underneath, that it would make me think, when I saw that I had hurt an innocent person, that my hatred caused suffering for someone who had done nothing to me. It might wake me up to my own condition. I might see my own guilt. I might, for the first time, realize that I cannot blame others for my vengeance. I might see their unselfishness and Jesus' forgiving attitude as a chance and invitation to a new life. I might be able to change sides. I might be able to put myself on the side of forgiveness instead of returning evil for evil.

That then is the meaning of Jesus' cross. This fits with the idea of mental health in our day. Counselors and psychiatrists have to be ready to take upon themselves some of the person's hostility. That is how to help the person get over it.

Mohandas Gandhi and Martin Luther King Jr. always said that they were not against the oppressing race. Gandhi was not against the British government and Martin Luther King Jr. was not against white people. Instead, they appealed to the oppressor's better self, trying to get you, the oppressor, to see the injustice of what is happening. Gandhi and King tried to help the oppressors stop, think, and change course. This is what Martin Luther King Jr. died trying to do. He was not, first of all, trying to obtain certain rights for African Americans. He was trying to bring white America to its senses. When in Birmingham, a few years ago, white America saw itself using dogs, fire hoses, and cattle prods on people, white America was called to self-awareness.

For modern humanity, it is very fitting to think of Jesus' death this way. Humanity is lost in vengefulness, lost in the vicious circle of hurt-for-hurt-for-hurt. But then God comes into that experience in the form of a perfectly innocent man who does no evil. He only tells the truth and is willing to suffer when people do not want to listen to him. So people, by their very nature, lash out against him and the reproach that they see in his holiness and purity. They hurt him. They kill him. But to the end he is forgiving, and he does not stay dead.

After it is over people realize it. The Roman soldier realizes that Jesus was an innocent person. Even Pontius Pilate realizes that Jesus is innocent. Judas recognizes it. Peter recognizes it. Paul later recognizes it. Each of them sees that "I had a part in killing this good person. He took our hostility on himself. He absorbed it both figuratively and literally to the death. Yet he was still forgiving, and he is still alive."

This view of the cross has had a long run in Christian history. Jesus had to die to do something about a warp in the human person. It is a meaningful and strong doctrine of the atonement. When we study this in seminary, I insist that students study it deeply and respectfully. But it is not enough to explain the cross. It doesn't explain many elements of the story, such as Jesus' teachings, his public life, or why he talked about himself as a king. But more important, it gives us the impression—which the Bible does not give us—that God is mostly concerned for my inner spiritual feelings.

Throughout the twentieth century, preachers such as Billy Graham and Norman Vincent Peale have told us that we ought to lead happy, wholesome lives. "You ought to be a mature person. You will not be happy if you do not set things right in yourself. Everything, even God, is here to help me have a good life in myself." This concern for my happy self is the quintessential American idolatry.

Jesus was not interested in this. Jesus told his disciples that they would have lives of conflict and self-denial. He did not say anything about maturity. He said that it is probably better to have your hand chopped off and to get into the kingdom than to be whole and not make it into God's purpose. The purpose of the cross had to be more than God's effort to call us to be mature.

There is another view that has been taken seriously in the Christian church. It found its strongest statement in the Middle Ages, in the age of the Christian empire, when all of Europe was called "Christendom." There were Christian kings and Christian emperors. It was a Christian civilization. It had Christian universities. Everyone was baptized. This society was a strictly governed society. It had taken over from Charlemagne and his ancestors the German idea of vengeance, that every crime has to be paid for and every disorderly act must be punished. This society had taken over from the Roman Empire ideas of justice and impartiality, as well as the notion that the law is above people, above the judge, and even above the king.

Medieval Christians, therefore, naturally thought about Jesus in this context. It was normal for them to think about God as a judge and to think about the law as demanding punishment for any misbehavior. That is the way it is in human life. So it must be that way before God. This law that demands punishment is even above God. So the only way God can satisfy this law is to sacrifice Jesus to it. Each and every one of us is guilty, and none of us can get ourselves out of this guilt. So we all have death coming to us. We have been judged. But somebody else, who did not have his or her own penalty to pay, could pay the penalty. That somebody is Jesus. Just as you can pay someone else's bills if you have enough money and are unselfish, so Jesus could give his life for the life that we should have given.

This is a very popular theme and meaningful way of talking about the cross in human history. In Christian history it has had a major place. We need to take it very seriously. We can also say, in a sense, that other martyrs, such as Martin Luther King Jr., paid the price for the sins of the society that they were trying to help.

But this doctrine also falls short. For one thing, the Bible does not give us a picture of a God who wants to punish somebody. The Bible does not depict the Father on one side and the Son on the other, with the Father wanting what is called "justice" and the Son favoring people instead. Moreover, this doctrine does not explain the entire story. Why did Jesus have his public career and teach as he did? Why did he have to be put to death in the manner that he was? Perhaps most problematic, why did Jesus teach that we too must bear a cross? So this particular way of explaining the meaning of the cross will not suffice either, although it is part of the picture.

There are still other views if we were to go back further into church history. There is the view that takes seriously what Jesus said about his life as a "ransom." So we can talk about how the devil has kidnapped us and how Jesus gave his life to free us. There is also the concept of wrestling with the powers of this world and the concept of sacrifice. But because these concepts come from further back in history, from a civilization very different from our own, it would be harder to see how they made sense then and what they say to us now, although in a theology course we would want to look at them more fully than can be done in a short sermon.

A truer meaning of the cross

For now, however, let's go to the story as John's gospel tells it since it contains a simpler answer that includes these other answers. But it is more human, more historical, and it must be truer.

> From then on Pilate tried to release him, but the Jews cried out, "If you release this man, you are no friend of the emperor. Everyone who claims to be a king sets

> himself against the emperor." When Pilate heard these words, he brought Jesus outside and sat on the judge's bench . . . Now it was the day of Preparation for the Passover; and it was about noon. He said to the Jews, "Here is your King!" They cried out, "Away with him! Away with him! Crucify him!" Pilate asked them, "Shall I crucify your King?" The chief priests answered, "We have no king but the emperor." Then he handed him over to them to be crucified. So they took Jesus. (John 19:12-16)

Whatever else we can say, we have to begin by saying that there had to be a cross because Jesus had frightened the authorities. Crowds followed him. He was identifying social evils and getting a hearing. There had been a parade into the city. There had been the cleansing of the temple, interference with people's ordinary religious rituals, interference with their economic life by setting loose all those sheep and bulls. He had let himself be called king, and later in John we are told that the label on the cross made it clear that the legal reason for his execution was that he was "King of the Jews" (19:19-22). Roman law required that when somebody was being put to death the reason should be explained publicly. Even today the theory behind the death penalty is that it will deter people. For the death penalty to deter crime, however, you have to say what crime it is that gets punished in this way. Therefore, when Jesus was put to death, the authorities said his crime was being "King of the Jews."

All too easily we might say today, "They had him all wrong! He did not want to be king. The kingdom he was talking about was not that kind of kingdom. They should not have felt threatened."

Jesus did not say that the authorities should not feel threatened by his teaching. Jesus said that he had committed no crime and had done no wrong. But he didn't say that he was trying to get out of trouble. He didn't say they misunderstood him when they thought that he was going to bring about a revolution. He could have said that, but he didn't. He would not have been crucified if he had made clear, as we often try to make clear, that he was not a troublemaker.

Second, whatever else Jesus' death means, there had to be a cross because Jesus said he was doing all of this in

God's name. He did not say that the cross was a good idea for improving Palestinian society. He did not say that the cross follows logically from some things we read in the Old Testament. That was the way the rabbis would have gone about it. He said simply, "In God's name: These things must not be. These things must be. This is the kind of life I must lead. This is the kind of life you must lead if you follow me." This rocked the boat because he did it in God's name.

Third, whatever else Jesus' death means, there had to be a cross because when this trouble came upon Jesus, he did not defend himself. He did not stick up for his rights. He didn't even demand a fair trial. He knew he would not get one. He was ready for injustice. He was ready to meet injustice forgivingly, sufferingly, nonviolently, and nonresistantly. He could have tried to escape. He could have staged a revolt or waged a holy war. He could have set the place on fire. But instead he went to the treatment that hateful people held out for him, and he did so without complaint.

Lastly, there had to be the cross because Jesus made no compromises. He didn't time his death so it would work. He didn't wait until he earned a hearing. He didn't choose a way of working that would not offend people. He didn't wait until the atmosphere was right and people were looking for what he had to offer. He didn't try to speak a language that people could accept without knowing how novel it was. He was uncompromising in the way that he stated God's judgment upon his society and God's promise to people in his society.

The meaning of the cross for Jesus' followers: Martin Luther King Jr.'s example

If that is what the cross meant for Jesus, what does it mean when he says that his followers will bear a cross and do the same? What does it mean that whoever is not ready to bear a cross is not worthy to be called his follower? What were his followers then to do?

We use the word *cross* in our hymns, in our piety, in our prayers, and in our pastoral language. But we use it too cheaply. We say that a person has to live with some sort of suffering in life: a sickness that cannot be cured, an unresolvable personality conflict within the family, poverty, or some other unexplainable or unchangeable suffering. Then we say, "That person has a cross to bear."

Granted, whatever kind of suffering we have is suffering that we can bear in confidence that God is with us. But the cross that Jesus had to face, because he chose to face it, was not—like sickness—something that strikes you without explanation. It was not some continuing difficulty in his social life. It was not an accident or catastrophe that just happened to hit him when it could have hit somebody else. Jesus' cross was the price to pay for being the kind of person he was in the kind of world he was in; the cross that he chose was the price of his representing a new way of life in a world that did not want a new way of life. That is what he called his followers to do.

That is what happened to Martin Luther King Jr. He represented a new way of life in a society that did not want that way of life. By and large, that kind of suffering, the price of nonconformity and nonresistance, is not happening to most Christians. It did not happen to Billy Graham or the National Council of Churches. It is not happening to Prairie Street Mennonite Church.

Second, what does Jesus' cross mean for what we call "Passion Week"? The cultural meaning of Easter in our society is a celebration of spring, when the world around us changes from brown to green, from dead and dull to colorful. The symbols we normally use for Easter are eggs and rabbits, which are ancient pagan symbols of fertility. Even the word "Easter" recalls the Anglo-Saxon goddess of spring.[3] The difference between the pagan worship of nature and the Christian concept of Easter is that spring is automatic. It always comes. By way of contrast, the resurrection only came after the cross.

We wonder in this happy time, when we are looking forward to new dresses, hats, and flowers, "Why did this social tragedy have to happen? Why did Chicago have to burn?

---

3. The Anglo-Saxon goddess of spring was named Ēostre. The only source we have for this is from the eighth-century church historian Bede. See Bede, *The Reckoning of Time*, trans. Faith Wallis (Liverpool, UK: Liverpool University Press 1988), 53–54.

Why did Martin Luther King Jr. have to die right now? It gets in the way of our celebration: the happiness, the fertility, the greening up again of nature."

This kind of escape from what Jesus' death really meant, recalled in Martin Luther King's murder this weekend, is possible for Christians whose faith revolves around the liturgy or the rituals, as that of the Sadducees did. It is possible for Christians, like the Pharisees in Jesus' time, to revolve their faith around having ideas right. It is possible for Christians, like the Romans of that time, to make faith a religion to keep society happy.

But for Christians who have promised to follow Jesus, who use the New Testament language that talks about discipleship and the cross, there can be no Easter before Good Friday. There can be no resurrection Sunday before being crucified on Friday.

We have to look beyond the church's walls to the turmoil of our time if we really care to know what it means to praise or to follow this Jesus who was ready to accept the cross. North American Christians, North American Mennonites—even Prairie Street Mennonites—have invested great effort in the past generations into becoming acceptable in society. We have worked at overcoming an attitude of separation in which our parents had been raised. This is partly good because it springs from a sense of responsibility to be out in the world with God's message. But part of this effort to be acceptable is dangerous, springing from a desire to fit in and be accepted, rather than be different and get mistreated. In our choice of residence, our way of dealing with money, our choice of social associates, and our pattern of going to church, most of us live most of the time more committed to the segregated, self-affirming, money-gathering patterns of the sick society that killed Jesus and killed Martin Luther King Jr. than we do committed to a vision of righteousness that would challenge and frighten our society, and would therefore give us occasion to suffer for it and to heal it.

Why do we need a savior? The guilt that killed Jesus and keeps on killing people like him is not only guilt somewhere on a heavenly account book that is kept up to date by a heavenly judge. Nor is it only in the troubled breast of the pious person. The guilt that killed Jesus and keeps on killing people like him is in the violent structures of a society that is based on pride, wealth, and power. That guilt is in the North American way of life. We need a savior because we are part of a system that justifies violence in its own defense. So the mayor of Washington, D.C., could say this morning that the city is in much better shape because he has ten thousand federal troops.[4] This violent structure of society is what Pilate, Caiaphas, and Peter were reacting to in different ways. President Lyndon Johnson and the National Guard are reacting to this cycle of violence as I speak. And this violent cycle is what discontented teenagers and looters are reacting to, all in their own way. Our own reaction is, "Why don't they all let us alone?" Or we hope that the unrest does not get as far as Elkhart, Indiana.

But what God did about it was not simply to hope to be left alone. What God did was come to us forgiving, giving hope, and threatening. The Son came expecting something to happen at God's own expense. Martin Luther King Jr. said that the cross is a forgiving, suffering, "community creating reality that moves through history."[5] That is what has to happen.

Let's close with a word from the book of Hebrews about the heroes of faith and the place of Jesus in this line of heroes.

> Others were tortured, refusing to accept release, in order to obtain a better resurrection. Others suffered mocking and flogging, and even chains and imprisonment. They were stoned to death, they were sawn in two, they were killed by the sword; they went about in skins of sheep and goats, destitute, persecuted, tormented—of whom the world was not worthy. They wandered in deserts and mountains, and in caves and holes in the ground. Yet all these, though they were commended for their faith, did not receive what was promised, since God had provided something better so that they would not, apart from us, be made perfect.

---

4. Following the assassination of Martin Luther King Jr. on April 4, 1968, many cities experienced days of rioting. Washington, D.C., experienced five days of rioting that nearly reached the White House on April 5, the day Yoder gave this sermon. At that time, Vice President Hubert Humphrey called in 13,600 federal troops, which included 1,750 federal Washington, D.C., National Guard troops, to help quell the riots in Washington, D.C.

5. See Martin Luther King Jr., *A Testament of Hope*, edited by James Washington (San Francisco: HarperSanFrancisco, 1986), 20.

Therefore, since we are surrounded by so great a cloud of witnesses, let us also lay aside every weight and the sin that clings so closely, and let us run with perseverance the race that is set before us, looking to Jesus the pioneer and perfecter of our faith, who for the sake of the joy that was set before him endured the cross, disregarding its shame, and has taken his seat at the right hand of the throne of God. Consider him who endured such hostility against himself from sinners, so that you may not grow weary or lose heart. In your struggle against sin you have not yet resisted to the point of shedding your blood. (Hebrews 11:35–12:4)

19

The Price of Discipleship[1]

Then Jesus said to him, "Someone gave a great dinner and invited many. At the time for the dinner he sent his slave to say to those who had been invited, 'Come; for everything is ready now.' But they all alike began to make excuses. The first said to him, 'I have bought a piece of land, and I must go out and see it; please accept my regrets.' Another said, 'I have bought five yoke of oxen, and I am going to try them out; please accept my regrets.' Another said, 'I have just been married, and therefore I cannot come.' So the slave returned and reported this to his master. Then the owner of the house became angry and said to his slave, 'Go out at once into the streets and lanes of the town and bring in the poor, the crippled, the blind, and the lame.' And the slave said, 'Sir, what you ordered has been done, and there is still room.' Then the master said to the slave, 'Go out into the roads and lanes, and compel people to come in, so that my house may be filled. For I tell you, none of those who were invited will taste my dinner.'"

---

1. Chapel sermon given at Fuller Theological Seminary on January 12, 1978. A transcription of the Fuller sermon has been available as an unpublished paper at Anabaptist Mennonite Biblical Seminary's library (AMBS), but had numerous errors where the audio was clearly misheard in the transcription. We have modified that transcription based on the audio from AMBS.

Now large crowds were traveling with him; and he turned and said to them, "Whoever comes to me and does not hate father and mother, wife and children, brothers and sisters, yes, and even life itself, cannot be my disciple. Whoever does not carry the cross and follow me cannot be my disciple. For which of you, intending to build a tower, does not first sit down and estimate the cost, to see whether he has enough to complete it? Otherwise, when he has laid a foundation and is not able to finish, all who see it will begin to ridicule him, saying, 'This fellow began to build and was not able to finish.' Or what king, going out to wage war against another king, will not sit down first and consider whether he is able with ten thousand to oppose the one who comes against him with twenty thousand? If he cannot, then, while the other is still far away, he sends a delegation and asks for the terms of peace. So therefore, none of you can become my disciple if you do not give up all your possessions." (Luke 14:16-33)

Our age and our culture have trained us to be sensitive about how to develop momentum in a movement or program, speech or meeting. Our self-awareness has been honed and trained to be careful, even if we didn't have this problem, to ask: Are you hearing me? How am I coming across? In our economics and in our sociology, we see movements and growth as having a self-sustaining dynamic that we must be careful about and cultivate so we do not cripple it. Don't lose the momentum.

In church and in mission, the competitive nature of North American church life has heightened our awareness of needing to attract people and not wanting to turn them off or have them change channels. We hear a speaker, we watch a television presentation, we even listen to our own preachers knowing that they realize we can turn them off. The speaker has no hold on our attentiveness—much less on our loyalty.

Our awareness of this mark of our culture may heighten our sensitivity to what Jesus is saying in the text above, especially the second paragraph of it. This text comes to us in the context of a story of growing momentum. Chapter 9 initiates a new segment of Luke's gospel. Jesus "set his face to go to Jerusalem" (v. 51). The whole story tilts; Jesus is on his way to a future climax.

In chapter 10, he sends out seventy people. They are told to put to everyone who hears them a decisive challenge. They must either be received or not received. That reception will matter for the "peace" of that family and that house into which they have come. They demanded decision, and a few days later they came back reporting success. They had had a hearing. Even the evil powers had listened to them. In chapter 12, so many thousands had assembled that they trod on one another.

In chapter 13, it is already becoming visible that the growing movement will have some kind of political implications. People come to Jesus wanting an opinion about an atrocity committed by Pilate at the Tower of Siloam, which some interpreters think must have been some kind of fort, representing resistance to the Romans. Not all the events and not all the teachings along the way directly reinforce this notion. But there is a dominant mood for those who read the middle of Luke as a story, rather than just a snippet at a time. There is a mood of growing momentum, growing membership, and growing audience.

Then a warning flag is raised. In the first paragraph of our opening Scripture, there are people who do not want to accept the invitation on its own terms. They ask for a rain check or to be excused. Then comes the text with which we are concerned. The "multitudes" are present. Jesus says, "Wait, don't decide lightly to follow me." He doesn't start with good news. He is not easing people into an initial commitment without their knowing where it will lead. He does not want them to be part of a "multitude" following him only because the multitude is attracted to part of his message or the fact that he is popular. There are numerous movements in our time that consciously do that. They present to the wider uninitiated public one picture of their message. Then once you start following, once you come to their meetings and live in their house, you find out there are dimensions you had not heard before. Jesus consciously avoids that. "I want you to know the bad news before you decide to follow me."

The public dimension of following Jesus

Jesus illustrates his warning with two political jokes. These are not ordinary parables in their style or structure. The ordinary parable deals with something typical. "A sower went out to sow." You don't ask, "Might I know the guy?" because it is universalizable. "A housewife lost a coin." You don't wonder who that might have been. But if you talk about a king who started a battle without thinking what it was going to cost, people might think, "Was there ever a king like that?" It happens that Herod had just done that. The same was true of a major building project. These two illustrations of someone being shamed or embarrassed because he had tried to do something he could not carry through were not imaginary or typical. They had happened. Men were laughing behind their beards at Herod because he had just done that. Jesus chose his illustration from public life. This is not typical of parables. It matters that he does that here.

I heard some good modern illustrations while in France because the French government had just done two of those things. They invested billions of francs in building an airplane, the Concorde. But the more it flies the more money the French will lose. The only reason they keep it is pride. They also spent billions to build, in northeastern Paris, an enormous public automated slaughterhouse, La Villette. All the little "mom-and-pop" butcher shops were about to be replaced by this enormous national combination slaughterhouse, cutting room, cold storage room, and packing room. Then they discovered that they had not made the conveyor belt to the right speed and had not gotten the right kind of refrigeration equipment. They had to tear the whole thing down.

If Jesus had been in France in 1973, he would have talked about the Concorde and La Villette, and anybody would have known what he was talking about. That is what he was doing with Herod's silly project. He chose to dramatize the issue of belief with examples from the public realm. He highlighted notorious political action. There is a public dimension to the commitment of the king who goes off to battle, and there is a public dimension to the shame. So, if you follow Jesus without knowing what you mean, there is a public dimension to the commitment. If you flop because you didn't mean it, there is a public aspect to the shame.

The meaning of the cross

It is important to note, in this context, that Jesus uses the word *cross*. For a long time I hadn't noticed that this usage, as we normally take it, is an anachronism. We primarily take it to mean what it could not have meant to its original hearers. If Jesus actually used the word *cross* at that time, what did the word itself mean to his listeners? To later readers there is no problem. We know about Jesus' cross, but Jesus' original listeners did not. If we sift through the parallel Gospels, we see that by this time Jesus was beginning to predict his suffering, but those predictions said he was going to be killed. They do not talk specifically about the cross. So, what does it mean here that Jesus refers to the cross before anybody knows exactly how he is going to die?

The meaning of the cross has to be drawn from the ordinary meaning that the word would have had before the fact of Jesus' death. It could not have meant "how they killed Jesus." The cross was not the way Jewish authorities killed anybody when they had the authority to kill people. The cross was the specific way in which the Romans executed insurrectionists, zealots, and revolutionaries. So, Jesus is saying, "If you are going to follow me, you will have to face the kind of suffering that is faced by those who are rejected by society for threatening its structures. Not just any old suffering, in general, not just any old kind of rejection, but the specific kind of rejection that faces the rebel will be your daily destiny if you want to follow me."

Perhaps this anachronism is explained by the fact that when Luke was writing he gave us a free translation. He may have updated the words he used so they could be understood by people long after the passion and for whom the reference to the cross did have a specifically Christian meaning. What you do with that suggestion depends on your understanding of how the Bible was written and edited. Luke chooses to tell the story in such a way that the more carefully we listen the more we are struck by the fact that Jesus tells his listeners, before his own death, that death of a specific kind—or at least readiness for death of that kind—will be their fate if they follow him.

Social estrangement as a price of discipleship

Central to the cost of following Jesus is social estrangement. Jesus does not talk about psychological suffering. He talks about difficulties with people. The parallel text in Matthew says, "I have come not to bring peace, but a sword" (Matthew 10:34). That social estrangement is located in the most intimate bonds of the nuclear family—between parent and child, sister and brother (vv. 35-37).

In later ethics, the family becomes the model of all social solidarity. In Martin Luther's *Catechism*, the family is the basis even of the state. In the Ten Commandments, where it says "Honor father and mother," Luther said that means, "Honor your prince because he is your father in the nation."[2] That's an understandable extension. It is that extension that applies when the choice is between following Jesus and following a nation, an ethnic group, or a social class, whether it be in war on any other kind of struggle. The solidarity into which one is born, the solidarity of one's nuclear or extended family, becomes representative for Western Christian thought of the duty to "my people" against other people.

Jesus says, however, that duty to "my people" as over against other people will no longer be our core obligation. Solidarities to those who are closest to us will now have to be called into question. In common ethical discourse, if you claim that it should be hard to justify the use of violence in self-defense or war, the dramatic way of responding is to ask, "Wouldn't you defend your mother? Wouldn't you defend your sister or your wife?" That's the place where reconfiguring social duties begins, according to Jesus. He does not

---

2. See Luther's *Large Catechism*: "Again, their princes and overlords were called *patres patriae* (that is, fathers of the country) to the great shame of us would-be Christians who do not speak of our rulers in the same way, or at least do not treat and honor them as such." See Martin Luther, *The Large Catechism of Martin Luther*, trans. Theodore Tappert (Philadelphia: Fortress, 1959), 28–29. Many later Mennonites adopted this same idea. For instance, in the seventeenth century, wealthy Mennonite leaders in Hamburg, Germany, taught their followers that secular rulers "were like fathers who corrected the wrongs of disobedient sons," quoted in Michael Driedger, *Obedient Heretics* (Aldershot: Ashgate, 2002), 121.

highlight the decisiveness of his call by making an emotional appeal or talking about how it ought to feel to follow him. He uses no imagery about loving him, caring, or being happy. Jesus dramatizes the decisiveness of his call by illustrating its social impact. It makes us relate differently to the people to whom we are bound the most closely by the ties of creation.

Although it is strong, this text is not atypical. It represents something we find elsewhere in the gospel story. There were people with excuses, like the "rich young ruler" who was kept from following Jesus. Jesus says, "Let the dead bury their own dead" (Luke 9:60) and "No one who puts a hand to the plow and looks back is fit for the kingdom of God" (9:62). This is mainstream gospel tradition.

Standard ways to avoid counting the cost

What should we do with this strand of the gospel story? There are some easy traditional ways to interpret it, or misinterpret it. One is to say that self-denial—the renunciation of self, self-esteem, or self-concern—is of value in its own right. Puritan and pietist disciplines have emphasized the duties of self-denial, as have various other Protestant traditions.

More recently, the whole notion of self-denial has been rejected. Therapeutic notions of self-fulfillment, self-assertiveness, or self-esteem have been used to correct the harmful impact of self-denial. Thus we stand in the midst of discussion about the sense in which self-denial is a value or that the self is of value in its own right. In some circles, there is a backlash against the self-esteem corrective. Bill Gothard's "Institute in Basic Youth Conflicts" movement tells us that self-affirmation is dangerous.

The self, however, is not Jesus' subject. It may be an important subject, but he is not talking about the self being of value in its own right, saying either yes or no to it, or how you should let it grow or prune it. He is talking about the kingdom. He makes the self an unimportant agenda. That's just the point. He doesn't care about whether you are happy. You should follow him. If you like that, you will be happy. If you don't like it, follow him anyway because that is the way. He refuses to get into the game of whether it is fun or fulfilling—our game about happiness and unhappiness.

A second way to interpret Jesus' warning is to take it as a matter of mood but not of reality. Jesus just means loosen your hold on things. Don't care so much about anything. He doesn't really mean give it up. For instance, he tells the rich young ruler to sell all he has and give the money to the poor, but some people claim that Jesus really does not care about the poor. He cares about the rich young ruler's spiritual liberty. If the rich young ruler can have a little more spiritual liberty, not be attached to his money, he can still keep it. They hold that Jesus was not committed to the poor. He cares about the rich person's spiritual experience. Therefore, you ought to continue to put your family first, just don't be too proud or hung up about it. You ought to continue to make money for yourself and not give it to the poor, as long as you feel that you could give it to the poor if you had to do so. So the radicality of being different in the real world is replaced by existentialism, which is a kind of inward analogue to what it would mean to be different in the real world.[3] It is about how you should feel about what you might do.

Another interpretation, for which I have considerable respect, but which is still not based on the text, is the place of the cross in pietist pastoral care. The retreat experiences and centers such as Keswick in Great Britain and the East Africa Revival Movement are samples of this. There is also some of this accent in Dietrich Bonhoeffer. Here the cross means inward brokenness. I bear the cross when I have faced the fact of my daily sinfulness and realize that I will never be able to be good. I will never save myself. I bring myself again and again to the cross as the dramatic symbol that God's readiness for me is never dependent on my performance, not even after conversion and sanctification. I need to internalize that in my personality and in my relations to people, to whom I must apologize and before whom I should humiliate myself in order to make the cross the shape of my inward life. This

---

3. Yoder notes as one of the striking samples of this Thomas Oden's *Radical Obedience: The Ethics of Rudolf Bultmann* (London: Epworth, 1965). Yoder adds that one could read the whole book without learning anything about what to do. The book regards all ethics as veiled evangelism, as if it is primarily about telling people that God ought to come first.

is true and beautiful as one element of Christian piety, but it is not what Jesus was talking about. We have to be honest with the story.

Mainstream Protestant pastoral care interprets the cross in relation to conflict and suffering, which is part of our faith in humanity. You have a difficult mother-in-law, a boss who is hard to work under, or a nagging medical malady. Each of us has a "cross to bear"—a sickness, an accident, or a catastrophe. We each have to bear suffering that is not the fruit of conflict or conflict that is not the fruit of discipleship. It is part of our common fate in this fallen world. Here again it is very important that pastoral care should tell people that God cares about their suffering. Suffering is meaningful under God's concern and in the body of Christian community. But that is not what Jesus is talking about.

The cross as the price for countercultural obedience

Jesus' cross was the price of his presence in a world that did not want what he was bringing. It was the price of his countercultural obedience. The cross of the disciples in this text is the same. He is saying, "You will have enemies. You won't destroy your enemies because that's not God's way and not my way. But they may destroy you. Don't follow me unless you are ready for that."

There is nothing in this passage to say why you will suffer or what it is you will suffer for. In later history, we became used to the idea that Christians sometimes suffer because of their theology, their form of worship, their doctrine, or their rituals. Christians in later history have, in fact, persecuted each other because of what they did with baptism, the episcopacy, or the doctrine of the Trinity. We have to make a positive effort not to read that understanding back into the text.

The offense Jesus' disciples were likely to suffer for was mostly in an ethical and social form. They would suffer because they would forgive people that the rest of society did not want forgiven, just as Jesus was scolded for doing. The disciples would call into question the nationalism of the right (that is, the establishment of the Sadducees) or the nationalism of the left (the national liberation front of the Zealots) because there are other ways of dealing with the Roman threat. They would be an offense because of what they did with their possessions. The grounds for persecution were not usually that it was not acceptable to have a high view of Jesus, but that these people were threatening the social order. A riot started in Ephesus because Paul took business away from the silversmiths. In Philippi he suffered because a slave girl was no longer usable to her masters. The offense hits the world where the world cares. The world does not really care how we celebrate the liturgy or whether we have bishops. It cares about what we do with our money, our bodies, our swords, and our land.

We have been told that Jesus was rejected because he thought he was the Son of God and that the earliest Christians were punished because they thought that as well. We have to do some careful historical unpeeling to avoid reading the story through the second, third, and fourth centuries. "Son of God," as in Jesus' temptation story, meant first of all, the King, the Anointed One, the one whom God destined to be used for specific purposes. "Son of God," as the second person of the Trinity or in the discussions of the "two natures" is a necessary later theological development, which we must care about and be faithful to, but it does not interpret what was going on here.

Jesus was unacceptable because he said he was the person God had sent to make a different story happen in the world. The disciples were not acceptable for the same reason.

Good news for the real world

For Jesus and for us this bad news should be part of the "good news." It should be part of the meaning of the joy and the victory that Jesus brings. This is not an anticultural warning. Jesus is not antisocial. He is not telling his people to be grumpy and pessimistic. He is not against joy or play, or even against this world's goods as long as we share them. There are those who think that Jesus' cross is antipolitical and anticultural, but they are the prisoners of puritan or pietist paternalism, against which they are rebelling.

Jesus is not against the real world. He does not oppose happiness and structure, or even power, family, and productivity. He is talking about what shape those things should have in the real world. He brings a new pattern for the real life of the real world—a new pattern that the world cannot tolerate because it is in the world, not because it is otherworldly or antiworldly. He says, "Love your enemies in this world because God does," in a world where people do not want to love their enemies. He says, "Forgive the offender in this world because God does," in a world that does not want to forgive the offenders. He says, "Share your bread, because God gave it to all of us," in a world that does not want to share bread. He says, "Upset the hierarchy, the slave is a brother of his master, the woman is of equal dignity to the man," in a world that wanted to save that hierarchy. He says, "Share your decision making because God, in the Spirit, is with all of us," in a world where decisions were supposed to be made by the people on top. He says, "Gather voluntarily because God's nature is such that God won't force you in," in a world where both religion and politics were coercive. He says, "Fulfill the law because God enables you to fulfill the law; I am the fulfillment of the law," in a world where what most people tried to do with the law was to redefine it so they could scrape through without much trouble.

The newness of Jesus is a new culture. It is a new society that has to be crucified because that is what the world does not want. Jesus is not teaching masochism or a martyr complex. This is neither defeatism nor withdrawal. This is the triumphant declaration of independence from the models of a fallen world culture in the name of God's original purpose.

There are some theological traditions that try to help us interpret this conflict as a conflict between redemption and creation. If we take Jesus' ethic too seriously, they say, we must take the ethic of creation less seriously. I can understand that position in the sixteenth century, and I talk about this approach respectfully in ecumenical discussions. But it does not help us to understand Jesus. He is talking about what God really wanted and nothing else. He is talking about the meaning of the created order restored in him in a fallen world.

What does all this mean for us?

Might Jesus' warning raise in our minds some questions about the usability of certain structures, certain media, and certain styles for communicating the gospel? Jesus could say what he said partly because he was a poor man with no office, who was talking to people who had voluntarily gone to the trouble to come to hear him. What does it do to our capacity to communicate the gospel when we have other warrants than that, other kinds of accreditation than that? Moreover, our communication ministry is based on charming the listener into tuning in to our channel instead of some other channel. Martin Marty is a theologian who has tried to take media seriously and concluded that we cannot preach the gospel on television.[4] We can do information. We can discuss entry-level issues. We can maintain a community of people who listen because they want to do so. We can do many good things related to the gospel, but we cannot preach the cross on television because people will change channels. That is too simple, but it makes the point we have to consider.

Are there certain ways of managing religious communication that are intrinsically incapable of saying what Jesus said? Are certain cultural and social forms not usable for the whole message? Are there certain places where this could not be said or could not be heard? The simplest example is that it was a mistake when, for a thousand years, Christians all over Europe thought they could force Jews to be baptized. There are places in Jewish culture today where that memory is still alive. There are places in the Near East where the memory of the forced baptizing of Muslims remains alive. Most of us would agree that was bad. But have we worked through the implications of why it was bad and how bad it really was?

Is it possible for a person with the power of an institutional chaplaincy—whether in military, hospital, factory, or prison chaplaincy—to say with integrity what Jesus said? Is it possible to say Jesus' revolutionary message at a country club prayer breakfast? Let's not think that government or prosperity itself is the issue. Is it possible to say it with populism strengthening your back? Is it possible to say it to an antigovernment audience, which is also a form of rabble-rousing, and still get the whole point across? The followers

---

4. See Martin Marty, *The Improper Opinion: Mass Media and the Christian Faith* (Philadelphia, PA: Westminster, 1961).

of Jesus, if they really follow him, are engaged in a story that means their whole life. That is talking about communication with integrity.

When we are among ourselves, when we are talking about the internal order of the Christian community, parish, or church-related agency, when we are in control of the forum, how do we use it? When we catechize new believers or persons who have responded to an invitation, how and when in that process do we repeat Jesus' warning? Where does that belong in an evangelistic crusade—before they come forward or after? Before they sign the card or after? Next week or in the process of moving from here to the church in which they will be lodged? In teaching the children of Christians, how do we avoid shooing them in or just "holding onto" the young people? How do we elicit and respect the doubts and reticence of those who really are not ready? What about those who really have not been moved by the Spirit to accept the invitation without condition? How do we engage those for whom it still matters that they not lose touch with their fields, their newly purchased oxen, or their newly married wife? Those are pretty basic elements of life that many candidates for membership are not ready to leave behind.

There is still another level of questions. Granted that our understanding of the matter might be clear and our readiness for unqualified obedience may be verified on the level of intention and beginnings, how do the structures of our church life reflect that readiness? Do we have educational counseling structures in the Christian community to help discern in our time and place where obedience must be willing to make enemies? If somebody does obey and does make enemies, where in our congregational life are the support structures for those who do suffer? In the church of which you are a part, what is the support structure for someone who would lose their job or family ties because of their faith?

Anything we really care about we can do. We think preaching is important, so we arrange to have a preacher. We think Bible study is important, so we find structures for that. If we think visitation is important, if we think overseas missions is important, if we think a neighborhood day care center is important, we will find a way to do it. What if we thought being crosswise with the world was important?

What structure would that take? Where is that in the committee framework of your parish? Where is our readiness for Jesus' stated conditions of discipleship to be real? The churches I have attended do not have committees for that. We do not expect that to happen, and it seldom does. Jesus did have a support system.

Mark 10:17-31 begins with the problem of money and then moves to the broader question of suffering. Jesus states, "How hard it will be for those who have wealth to enter the kingdom of God!" (v. 23). Peter responds by saying, "We have left everything and followed you" (v. 28). Then Jesus says: "Truly I tell you, there is no one who has left house or brothers or sisters or mother or father or children or fields, for my sake and for the sake of the good news, who will not receive a hundredfold now in this age—houses, brothers and sisters, mothers and children, and fields with persecutions—and in the age to come eternal life " (vv. 29-30).

There is an alternative community. There is even an alternative family. There is a new place to be family, to be home. Jesus' call is not apocalyptic. He is not calling us to go off the end of the system we know. He does not call us to loneliness. It is not otherworldly or antiworldly; it is new-worldly. It is a new reality, but with persecution, with the cross. The gate is narrow. Not many people take that road. But what it leads to is the kingdom, even a hundredfold in this life.

We are afraid to introduce in our church structure, our preaching, and our counseling processes any seriousness about the cross. This is partly because we do not really believe that beyond the narrow gate there is the kingdom. It is partly because we do not really believe that beyond the cross there is resurrection and that even in this life, beyond dying, there is rising to newness of life. We also do not do that because we think we live in a better world. We live, after all, in Christian America. What Constantine did not do, Cromwell and Carter have done. They have given us a society in which Jesus' warning does not apply.

We have many reasons not to believe actively that Jesus' word is for us. I suggest that you keep testing those assumptions. We should look in faith to what it might mean if—even after Christianity came to full predominance in the Western world, even after political rights, religious liberties, freedom of movement, and cultural prosperity have made it a tolerable thing to be Jesus' followers—it might still be the case that what he said was not only for the first century, or for the first three, or for heroic missionary places like China and Afghanistan, but for our time and our place. Was the cross Jesus talked about bad news that frightens us or was it the price of the good news?

20

Peace as Proclamation[1]

Peace used to be a promise. In the Old Testament vision and in the song of the angels at Bethlehem, peace was a mark of the Messiah. Yet somehow that promise was not true. We do not yet have peace. The traditional Jewish answer to Christian claims is that if Jesus had been the Messiah he would have brought peace, but he did not.

In the early twentieth century, peace was thought to be a human achievement or performance. For Mennonites and peace churches more broadly, "the peace position" meant, at least more visibly than anything else, the refusal of military

---

1. This sermon was preached on December 2, 1977, at Anabaptist Mennonite Biblical Seminary, whose library has archived the audio. We are grateful to Aaron Woods for transcribing this sermon. Because Yoder preached this message to a mostly Mennonite audience, he took for granted that they shared his convictions about nonviolence. In this volume, Yoder does not make his biblical case for this commitment. That will come in volume two, *Revolutionary Christian Citizenship*. We include it here because it showcases Yoder's conviction that Christians should not be ashamed of the radical dimensions of the Christian walk, but should proclaim them boldly as part of the good news. What Yoder says here about his peace convictions can be said equally about a variety of topics discussed in this volume. For a very good, easy to read introduction to Yoder's biblical case for pacifism, see *He Came Preaching Peace* (Eugene, OR: Wipf and Stock Publishing, 1985).

service. That was an identifiable position. It is something that we ought to do. It is something that we can do, and it is something that many of us did in World War I and World War II. This experience has defined the identity of peace church people.

Defined as refusing military service, the peace position not only made sense out of our present, it even made sense of our past. We were able to see the history of Mennonite migrations as justified and motivated by the peace position. We were able to see our social strangeness, our sense of not being with the rest of the world, as making sense because of the peace position. We were able to see our separateness from the English-speaking urban culture as proper because it is part of renouncing the dominant culture's violence and militarism.

Then there was a time when peace was not simply a performance; it was a prophecy. It said something clear to the world. The civil rights movement and the movement against the Vietnam War had a serious, relevant, and understandable social critique. The peace position was something that had to be and could be said. It could also be heard and recognized. The appropriateness of this position was reinforced by the openness of elite persons in wider society who affirmed that this inherited position made sense and was relevant. The message was respectable. It was even needed and appreciated.

Peace as a problem

Today, however, we probably have to confess that peace is now less a promise, less a performance, and less a prophecy. Peace is more of a problem. The situation is less rewarding today. There is no draft to make sure that every family thinks about military obligations. We have no handles on the Pentagon and cannot figure out where the decisions are made. Even a president who runs with a platform of ultimate nuclear disarmament begins by affirming the usability of the neutron bomb as a basis for negotiation. We are increasingly aware of the complexity of the world in which we wanted to have a peace position.

We know enough political science, sociology, and even psychology to know that the rejection of military service was at best the tip of the iceberg, and to doubt whether the rest of the iceberg is still there. We also doubt whether rejecting military service is really enough to be sure that we even have a peace position. What about the other ways we use power? What about the other ways we affirm national loyalties? What about the other ways in which we are conformists? Because we are more aware of the complexity of what it would mean to have a peace position, peace is more problematic. We are also more aware of our complicity. We see ourselves as part of the problem. We are aware, as our parents were not, that the way we are housed and the way we transport ourselves are part of the oppression of a globally unjust society. We are not sure what we can do to change it. Peace is a problem because we see more clearly the limits of the simple answers from which we got our identity—an identity imposed upon us by the draft and a different social scene.

Separation from the world used to have a simple meaning for Mennonites. Our separateness was related to the urban/rural tension, to the fact that we spoke German in an English-speaking culture, and to other elements of social style. All of this once seemed to fit with our peace position. Conformity was conformity to power. Separateness was separateness from the power struggle. Now, however, we see our separatism as an embarrassment, perhaps irresponsible, sometimes irrelevant, and not really as freeing us from complicity in the world's power struggles.

We feel very different about being right. A minority that is persecuted and feels their position is right may short-circuit some big intellectual problems or may be unaware of their position's limitations. There is, however, a certain psychological naturalness to feeling at home in a position for which one is struggling and suffering. But when we stop struggling and suffering for a position, then we begin to feel embarrassed about claiming to be right. Don't we want to be a little more pluralistic in ecumenical relations? Don't we want to recognize that there are flaws in our own position as well? Even the notion that this is a position, and that it is right, which was so evident a generation or more ago, is questionable to many of us just in terms of etiquette. Why should we think we are right? Why should we have any authorization to commend to others a position that we ourselves only hold because we are born into it? Shouldn't we be more ecumenical, which would mean recognizing that other people are right, too? Shouldn't we be polite, which might mean talking as if other people were right more than we are? Isn't that a more humble way? This doubt about our rightness is a good way to start a conversation. It might even be true that we have more to learn than to teach. That makes the peace position a problem.

Peace as a proclamation

But I suggest that we remind ourselves that peace should be as it was in Isaiah's words: a proclamation. It is a gospel message. It is not something that we have to prove we are right about by arguing biblically or in any other way. It is something that is given us in proclamation and to be proclaimed.

One of the gospel's fundamental characteristics—especially as the Protestant Reformation has taught us—is that we are not right because we are right, because we can prove it, or because we can achieve it. We are made right. We are made righteous. We are justified by faith. The rightness of a peace position does not rely on our being good pacifists or making peace. The rightness of this position is its derivation from who God is and what God has done in Jesus. Therefore, some of our introspection and some of our guilty conscience should be set aside if we really believe the gospel is rooted in itself and not in our good record.

Peace is proclamation in the sense that we should talk not first of all about a social strategy for making the world a little less lethal, but about a victory already won. The gospel is about something that has already happened. It needs to make ripples. It needs to work down through the centuries. But the meaning of the gospel is not these ripples themselves. The meaning of good news is a victory already won. Our sense of what is going on in peace witness, in peace lobbying, in teaching, in rediscovering the meaning of reconciliation in family structures and every other level of our experience, would be very different if we saw peace as a proclamation and not a problem. Instead of thinking of an almost impossible task to be accomplished, we should root peace in the victory that has already been won. That Christ is Lord is not up to us to achieve but only to reflect.

Peace is proclamation also in another sense: that we ought to see our action not simply as morality but also as communication. That is, we should ask about a deed not simply, "Are its goals and intentions right?" We should also ask, "What does it say? What does it preach?" Jesus said of his disciples that they were to be visible like a city on a hill (Matthew 5:14). The way they were going to be different was not simply that they were going to perform different things and achieve different results. Their being different was going to say something to the world. If I love my enemy, that preaches something about what God does with God's own enemies. We need to understand the meaning of ethics as preaching, that is, behavior that communicates God's nature. We do not simply ask whether a deed hurts anybody, whether it keeps or breaks the rules, or whether it implements a long-range process that will be good for a maximum number of people. That is worth doing as well. But if ethics is also preaching, then we will ask about our deed, "What does this say God is like?" That is why we must love our enemies. Our deed must say to the enemy that God loves him or her.

Finally, to say that peace is proclamation would mean that we need to remind ourselves much more often than we do that the peace witness is not a sectarian appendix to Christian truth. It was often thought and sometimes rather convincingly explained that Mennonites are real Christians except that they have a little extra baggage. They believe everything that a Christian ought to believe, but in addition they have nonresistance and nonconformity. That is the source of the embarrassment already mentioned.

Nonresistance and nonconformity, if they make any sense, cannot be separated from all Christian truth. They cannot be separated from the nature of the God who loves enemies and rebellious creatures. They cannot be separated from Christian understandings of the nature of human persons and what it means for them to be whole and reconciled. Peace witness and the rejection of violence cannot be separated from the Christian understanding of the church. It is inseparable from the meaning of membership, the meaning of decision, and the meaning of covenant. The peace witness is not separable from the nature of atonement, from what it takes for sin to be set aside and persons to come to wholeness within themselves, within the community, within history, and between the self and the Creator. There is no peace witness apart from an understanding of the nature of God's victory that enables us to be the suffering servant, the enemy lovers, the forgivers, and the second-mile goers that we are called to be, because that is the way our Lord was.

The slain Lamb is the meaning of history

In Revelation 4 and 5, the elder John sees the heavenly court room. The one seated on the throne has in his hand a sealed scroll, which signifies the seal to the unknowable inscrutable quality of history. John does not know why he is imprisoned on Patmos. He does not know why the Romans are still running the world. He doesn't know why the church is not triumphant. That "not knowing" is dramatically symbolized by the sealed scroll. Neither do the elders around the throne know the meaning of history or what they are waiting for in the heavenly court room. So John weeps.

Then he is told that there is an answer to this question. There is one who has the authority to break the seals and unroll the scroll and thereby read the meaning of destiny. That one is the slain Lamb. There is no mention of the name Jesus, no mention of the title Messiah. But this is a proclamation that what has happened in the event of the cross, what has happened in the living out of suffering love—through the suffering servant—is the true meaning of ongoing history. In this history the Lamb is worthy of all kinds of praise because in his sacrifice he has opened up space for a new people who are called out from all the peoples of the world. The Lamb has made it possible that there should be a new peace, thanks to the gift of his victory.

21

Discipleship as a Missionary Strategy[1]

A number of North American Mennonites have had the privilege of visiting the Wheathill colony, a Hutterian "Bruderhof" in the west of England. For those who feel that Mennonite discipleship is a matter of church history, who wonder whether it is possible for a small and largely rural church to "hold its ground," the example of this colony and its three sisters in Paraguay is both a lesson and a reprimand.

After the First World War there began in Germany an experiment in community living that grew out of some intellectuals' conviction that a radically new approach to life and to economic reality was the only answer to the social and spiritual chaos of modern Europe. The leader of this community was Eberhard Arnold. Though the beginning was an

---

1. "Discipleship as a Missionary Strategy," *The Christian Ministry* (January–March 1955): 26–31. Though this essay addresses themes that are central to volume 3 of this book series, it is included here to make clear Yoder's conviction that the radical Christian discipleship to which we are called takes place in the context of the Christian community and on behalf of its witness to the world. Yoder's biblical case for many of the congregational practices that he assumes in this chapter is made in volume 3, *Real Christian Fellowship*.

entirely original idea, Dr. Arnold later became acquainted with the history of the Hutterian movement, visited the North American Hutterians, and received their fraternal blessing. This is the only organic link between the original Hutterian movement and the Wheathill and Paraguay Bruderhof colonies.

Driven from Germany by Hitler in 1936, the group found refuge in southern England, only to be obliged to leave for Paraguay at the beginning of World War II because of their German nationality. During their brief stay in England, a number of English citizens joined them, two of whom stayed behind to dispose of their property. Before they could leave, however, these two were joined by forty more and, after consultation with the group in Paraguay, it was decided that a new property should be found and a colony formed that would stay in England. This is the Wheathill Bruderhof, which now has a population of one hundred adults and one hundred children. The group which went to Paraguay, after first finding a home among the Mennonites, now has three colonies with a total of some seven hundred members. Some fifty persons yearly join the Wheathill group.[2]

The first reaction of a statistically-minded North American is to reflect that a movement that in thirty years can have nearly 1,000 members, starting from nothing, in the face of confiscation of their property and forced migration, is a more successful mission enterprise, percentagewise, than any modern Mennonites can show. But the Hutterians do not live as they do in order to evangelize effectively. They live and witness as they do because they are convinced that it is the only way to answer the Lord's call to obedience, and this commitment is in itself the only sound foundation for evangelism. Even though the Hutterian Brethren themselves

---

2. Since their founding in the 1920s, the Bruderhof have grown to over 2,500 people living in ten different communities on three different continents (North and South America, and Europe). They should be distinguished from the Hutterites, who are a much older group of Anabaptists. For a brief but helpful overview see Donald F. Durnbaugh, "Bruderhof," in *Encyclopedia of Community: From the Village to the Virtual World*, ed. Karen Christensen and David Levinson (Thousand Oaks, CA: Sage Publications, 2003), 104–7.

rightly see the problem in another light, it will be justifiable for us to analyze their approach as a missionary strategy, for it is undeniably the most effective strategy to be observed in our century in any of the churches of the Anabaptist tradition.

An invitation to a changed life

The evangelistic appeal of the Hutterians is not an invitation to change churches or religions, but to change lives. The utter break with the old life is rendered visible and irrevocable by the fact that it involves giving up private property and going to live in the Bruderhof. This is how the Hutterians apply Jesus' invitation to "leave all and follow me" in our times. We may justly refuse to agree that the rejection of private property has the status of a moral absolute, but it is wrong to hide behind this justified refusal and to go on living in conformity to North American individualistic materialism.

North American evangelists often interpret the gospel invitation to follow Jesus as forsaking tobacco, lipstick, or the movies. It is seldom proclaimed clearly that it means a whole way of life and a whole way of thinking about material goods. Evangelists have a tendency, right in one sense, to make the gospel easy. Yet Jesus' words about counting the cost and planning to bear the cross (Luke 14) teach, and Anabaptist and Hutterian histories confirm, that the proclamation that makes plain the gospel's severest demands is the same one that makes plainest its good tidings. Is an evangelism that avoids mention of nonresistance, stewardship, and right living in all its details good evangelistic technique? Or is it an effort to please people, which will, if successful at all, flood the church with tepid Christians who feel it to be an imposition when the church asks anything of them?

Radical stewardship

The Bruderhof pattern has a second advantage: it facilitates radical stewardship. The simple life and the giving of surplus are much easier to administer where there is a common kitchen, a common purse, and a common clothing supply, than where sixty families must each manage an income and a household—each providing its own transportation, food, housing, and clothing, paying its own income taxes, and making its own decisions about saving and giving. However conscientious the sixty families may be, their stewardship will in many cases be less efficient and in some cases more self-indulgent than if it were done together in the fellowship.

The strong case for the Bruderhof system has nothing to do with the advocacy of communism or socialism, which, being imposed on non-Christians, are often quite inefficient. It has to do with Christian fellowship. It would require a degree of devotion and willingness to submit to the fellowship that not all of us have, but that is an argument for and not against the proposal. Meditate for a minute on how you would like to submit to the judgment of fellow Christians as to whether you need a new shirt, how long you should work, how comfortably you should travel, and how you should educate your children. Then ask whether your initial negative reaction is biblical.

Evangelism directed toward people of goodwill

Evangelism as the Hutterians practice it, through correspondence, publication, and visitation, is not an effort to persuade into faith people who know what God wants and refuse to do it. It is not an attempt to convince people of the existence of God or the imminence of God's judgment. Nor does it seek to convict people of sin who are content with themselves. Rather, they seek out those individuals who, through their own thinking, are generally out of reach of the church's language, come to be dissatisfied with life, and are looking for a better answer.

Evangelism is thus directed not at the children of Christian families and people on the fringe of the church. It is directed at people of good will among the pagans who know nothing of the gospel message, but are ripe to receive it. There is much to be said for this view of evangelism biblically (for example, Cornelius, the Ethiopian, Dionysius), theologically, historically, and psychologically. This approach requires some things that modern mass evangelism tries to get along without, including the time to work with individuals personally, the backing of a fellowship of Christians who have life abundantly and let it show, and the capacity to meet people on their own level without requiring them to learn pious language before being able to understand. Since the type of person most likely to receive such a message is often capable of independent thinking and ignorant of Christian thought, one must often deal with very muddled self-made theories and principles spun by the mind in its effort to understand oneself without revelation.

As was the case in the very first years of the Anabaptist movement, this type of evangelism appeals to independent thinkers, often middle-class tradespeople, professional people, engineers, white-collar workers, and intellectuals. This means that the group is enriched constantly by the influx of new people with such abilities. At the same time, the fact that a farm cannot use all these abilities shows one of the limitations of the purely rural Bruderhof system.

The fellowship as the basis for evangelism

The basis of evangelism is *koinonia*, the fellowship of those who seek the will of Christ together. The community's decisions are made prayerfully by the members' unanimous agreement, be it a matter of financial organization, work planning, or church discipline. Missionaries are guided week by week in their travels by the fellowship at home. The fact of Christian fellowship as a real sharing of all life's concerns, which the prayer meeting, Sunday school class, and small group movement try to provide, is expressed by the whole pattern of Bruderhof living. Tenth-generation Mennonite Christians with a solid tradition of family-centered rural community life can get along without a vital experience of Christian fellowship because family ties are a fair substitute. But for rootless and friendless modern Western individuals whose only home is a rented apartment, whose only society is party-going or business contacts, and whose deepest feeling is one of loneliness in the midst of the city's crowds, no aspect of the Hutterian witness is more appealing than the existence of a fellowship of Christians willing to accept them as one of their own, share with them their wealth and poverty, and treat them as people and no longer as things.

Restoring baptismal commitment

Throughout Mennonite history, a major cause of spiritual decline in times of toleration, apart from the possession of wealth, has been the too-easy integration of the children of Christians into the church. As long as persecution continued, it was clear to everyone what was involved in confessing one's faith. The request for baptism retained its character of dangerous and conscious commitment to a break with the world. With persecution gone it became easier for a young person to stay in the church community, which was also that person's family, than to leave it. Baptism became an act of conformity rather than a break with the world. Young people, ever so serious and well meaning, could not really know what commitment was involved. Two generations of such practice, coupled with a lack of discipline, suffice to render any church lukewarm.

It would be attacking the problem backward to go looking for a "moral equivalent of persecution" in order to keep the church alive. There are, however, measures which can be taken, and which should be taken for their own sake to restore the original content of the commitment of baptism. The first is to have a clear and demanding standard of Christian life, enforced by discipline, so that no one thinks that ordinary decent behavior, "as good as anyone else," is enough. The Hutterians, like the Amish, apply 1 Corinthians 5:11 literally. Aspects of stewardship and simplicity should be dealt with by discipline just as clearly as military service.

It is just as important to avoid confusing Christian nurture and evangelism. This means we should avoid pressuring young people to follow the path of least resistance and remain within the group. This is the point where North American Mennonites have the most to learn from the Hutterians, and at this point there comes to light the basic difference between a strategy of love and a strategy of fear (see 1 John 4:18). A strategy of fear, aiming at survival (in spite of Matthew 10:39), seeks first of all to "hold on to the young people" by making baptism easy, sheltering them from outside contacts, encouraging them to be conscientious objectors with or without conviction, and building ties of family, community, and vocation that make it difficult, if not impossible for baptism to be understood as a break with everything.

Where there is no real freedom to make a commitment, the commitment is worth little more from a twelve- or fifteen-year-old than it would be from an infant in a Lutheran baptism when the godparents renounce the world, the flesh, and the devil. A strategy of love, on the other hand, has sufficient trust in the Spirit's work and in the attraction of true discipleship to risk waiting for the decision to request baptism until it comes uncoaxed from an adult who knows what the choice means. Whereas this attitude is open to the reproach, "You make it easier for young people to leave the church than to stay," the probability is that this strategy of love works better at "holding on to the young people" than the strategy of fear that sets out with that purpose.

Attaining this goal in the apparently closed community of a Bruderhof requires a carefully thought through program of education. The school is, indeed, one of the most remarkable things at Wheathill. Better than in the public schools, children are taught to become individuals and to think out their own answers. They are taught to use money, which no one in the colony handles. After primary school they go into apprenticeship or advanced education away from the Bruderhof, where they learn the joys and temptations of being one's own boss and where they acquire skills and friendships that would enable them to live better (in terms of wealth and social esteem) in "normal society" than in the Bruderhof. Then if they decide to return to the Bruderhof for life, as they usually do, they know what they are accepting and what they are rejecting. They also have more to offer the brotherhood in terms of skills and personality than if they had fearfully been kept at home in an attempt to preserve them from the world. In a period of toleration or even prosperity, the commitment of adult baptism retains its original meaning and the first principle of Anabaptism is safeguarded as in no other way.

This concern for the freedom of young people to make their own commitments does not mean a sacrifice of Christian nurture. It puts nurture in its proper perspective by separating it from evangelism. In practice the two may coexist, but in concept they are distinct. The parent's responsibility before God is to lead their children to become a mature, honest, informed, independent, industrious human being capable of making a contribution in the world. This includes informing them of basic moral principles that are valid whether or not they are believers and informing them, more by deed than word, that one can follow those principles in the abundant life of the Spirit. This education gives them the necessary basis for a Christian commitment and unavoidably creates a certain leaning, but it will not make the decision for them nor keep them from becoming acquainted with other possibilities.

In one sense it may be said that the difference between Calvinism and Anabaptism is that Calvinism considers every child of Christian parents as destined to be Christian, whereas Anabaptism maintains the possibility that a child of Christians may reject the faith. This difference needs to be built into the foundation of a Mennonite philosophy of education. Whereas Calvinism, aiming to produce 100 percent Christians, makes some proud puritans and some rebels, Anabaptism leaves the percentage to God and aims to produce either disciples who can stand on their own commitment or non-disciples who will make an honest contribution to society because of their solid moral education.

The Spirit will lead us

Without taking the space to dot all the i's and draw all the morals, we have seen what it means to say that discipleship is a missionary strategy. I have used the example of the Hutterian Brethren (which incidentally does not correspond with the North American Hutterians) to illustrate an attempt to apply the Anabaptist viewpoint today. Our guide remains, however, not the Anabaptist or the Hutterian example, but the life of the Spirit as revealed in the New Testament, to which every person is called and every disciple is committed. May that same Spirit reveal again in our day, as God has in the past, God's will for church order, education, stewardship, and evangelism.

22

God Keeps My Commitment[1]

> I know not why God's wondrous grace
> To me He hath made known . . . ,
> I know not how this saving faith
> To me He did impart . . .
> I know not how the Spirit moves,
> Convincing us of sin . . .
> I know not what of good or ill
> May be reserved for me . . .
> I know not when my Lord may come,
> At night or noonday fair . . . ,
> But I know Whom I have believed,
> And am persuaded that He is able
> To keep that which I've committed
> Unto Him against that day.[2]

This gospel song has enshrined for us one of the monumental mistranslations of the King James Bible: "He in whom I have believed is able to keep what I have committed to Him" (2 Timothy 1:12).[3] This is how it has long been read.

---

1. Originally given May 26, 1963 as the commencement address to the graduating class of Anabaptist Mennonite Biblical Seminary.

2. This hymn, "I Know Whom I Believe," was written by Danielle W. Whittle in 1883.

3. Yoder has slightly rearranged the order of the King James Version in this quote.

The original language reads more simply and clearly: "He is able to keep my deposit" or "my trust." Both translations are possible. "My deposit" may mean either "what God has entrusted to me" or "what I have entrusted to God." But use of the words and the thoughts of this verse elsewhere suggest that Paul means the former.

Our commitment is God's gift to us and not ours to God

On this difference hangs all that matters in how we understand our "commitment" as servants of the will and Word of God. Is this essentially the decision of humanity—in this case Paul—to commit something to God, a decision which could have turned otherwise, or is it the decision of God, who has entrusted to us a task that takes our lives out of our own hands and which alone can give them meaning? Is it the human person who deigns to trust God, or is it the other way around? Is the "commitment," which we believe God is able to keep, a promise we have made to God or one God has made to us?

It is not only the seventeenth-century King James translators who have made us think the former more appropriate, as if we had done the Lord a favor by trusting God with some precious possession, and then paid God a compliment by believing the Lord capable of taking good care of it for a while. This human-centered attitude is fostered by the contemporary evangelistic mindset, which seeks to make God attractive to humans, rather than humans acceptable to God. It is fostered by the apologetic stance in much theology and philosophy of religion, which agrees with unbelievers that humans may somehow judge God's credibility. It is fostered by religious advertising as it labors to convince people on the street that they need a trustworthy God in the same way that they need a more reliable car.

To this perversion of the gospel, the only fitting response is a resounding "No!" God is not reliable, if by that we mean that the Lord can be counted on to run our errands and otherwise "persuade" us that God is able to watch our baggage while we go on with the important work. God's faithfulness is that God is true to God's own self, not to what we expect. Amos warned that the encounter with God is not necessarily a reassuring experience: "Why do you want the day of the

LORD? It is darkness, not light; as if someone fled from a lion, and was met by a bear; or went into the house and rested a hand against the wall, and was bitten by a snake. Is not the day of the LORD darkness, not light, and gloom with no brightness in it?" (Amos 5:18-20).

God's coming among us to fulfill the Old Testament promise has always surprised those who were waiting for the Messiah. In the mere suggestion that it might be humanity's prerogative to decide whether to be "persuaded" of God's ability, as in the song quoted above, lies the seed of all the humanistic heresies of our age.

It is a reminder of the priority of grace when Paul tells us that the trust over which God stands watch is not our salvation that we have entrusted to God, but the apostolic ministry that God has laid upon us. The salvation we must trust the Lord for is not God's trustworthiness in assuring our eternal destiny, but our faithfulness in carrying out our present task. What God has called us to, "not according to our works but according to his own purpose and grace" (2 Timothy 1:9), is not the joy of forgiveness, but the holy calling. This calling invites us to join "in suffering for the gospel, relying on the power of God" (v. 8). The background of Paul's confession of confidence is not, as in the hymn I quoted, his ignorance about the mysteries of God's working. It is the temptation to "be ashamed" in the face of the suffering that his ministry entailed.

> Do not be ashamed, then, of the testimony about our Lord or of me his prisoner, but join with me in suffering for the gospel, relying on the power of God, who saved us and called us with a holy calling, not according to our works but according to his own purpose and grace. This grace was given to us in Christ Jesus before the ages began, but it has now been revealed through the appearing of our Savior Christ Jesus, who abolished death and brought life and immortality to light through the gospel. For this gospel I was appointed a herald and an apostle and a teacher, and for this reason I suffer as I do. But I am not ashamed, for I know the one in whom I have put my trust. (2 Timothy 1:8-12)

Therefore, let this be our first lesson. Our commitment is the apostolic charge laid upon us. The claim it has upon us is founded not upon the clarity or sincerity of our devotion to

God but upon the priority of God's coming to us. The testing our commitment must face is not our doubting whether God has truly called us or whether we have truly believed, but the world's hostile response. "For he has graciously granted you the privilege not only of believing in Christ, but of suffering for him as well" (Philippians 1:29).

Let it be our prayer that despite the egocentric mentality of our society we might understand our service to God, the world, and the church not as the gift of ourselves to God but as God's gift to us.

Our commitment is to Jesus' story

Our text continues: "Hold to the standard of sound teaching that you have heard from me . . . Guard the good treasure entrusted to you" (2 Timothy 1:13, 14). What has been entrusted to us is a "standard of sound teaching." Timothy was a man of many gifts. Paul was even more blessed with great capacities of will and spirit. Yet when Paul speaks of the "treasure" put in his charge, as "herald, apostle, and teacher" of the gospel, it is not his "gifts," his theological insight, his missionary zeal, his good heritage, or his capacity for mystical experience. It is a deposit—something passed on from person to person, from other people to Paul to Timothy—that he considers a sacred trust.

We shall never be done stretching to gauge the full weight of the fact that Christians are first and foremost custodians of a story. More than we want to admit, the challenge to Christian faithfulness is posed by those who would make of it something other—something better in their minds—than a story. The philosopher in us would rather find enshrined in the story some deeper insights that would be equally true if the story were not told. The counselor or the preacher, both seeking to be existential interpreters, would transform the story into the effect that its telling has on the lives of those who hear. The artist in us would transpose it into the soundings of ritual recitation. The churchman in us would place it on the pedestal of a growing church program. The devout disciple in us would seek to reproduce the story in our own life. All of this is right and good. Yet once again the good may be the worst enemy of the best.

Over and over again God's people have let themselves be told that one or another of these necessary and good reflections of the story—the exegesis, the ritual retelling, the soothed soul, or the lubricated community—is the story itself. The task of theology is to refuse to find a higher or deeper, a more simple or a more attractively complicated grasp of God's grace and glory than the factuality of the gospel events. Should it be that this witness provides the key to the only intellectually satisfying view of the world, we should be the last to be surprised. But that is not why we proclaim it. We do not tell the old, old story because it satisfies our longing; we tell it because it is true.

The story's effect on a man or woman who really hears it is to call forth a response of dedication. Whether this actually happens—whether the rich young ruler leaves his wealth and the farmer his newly purchased team, the fisherman his nets and the tax collector his cashbox—is the test of whether the story has been truly understood. Where there is no total commitment to the gospel, there has been no total liberation by the gospel. Where there is no fellowship or growth in grace, it is not clear that there has been grace at all. But beware: not even the genuineness and the depth of Christian commitment can paraphrase and replace the story into which the committed one is seized up. The genuineness of evangelical commitment lies not in the heart of the devoted believer. It cannot be confirmed or undermined by delving into his or her subconscious. The guarantee of Christian commitment is objective, not subjective. Paul boasts not "that I have believed" but of "whom I have believed."

Let this be our second lesson. We are not committed to our commitment. We are being dragged along in the conquering hero's triumphant procession, to use imagery from Colossians 2. If we seek to keep the commitment pure, it must be by keeping the story straight. No amount of intellectual depth or anti-intellectual enthusiasm, neither orthodoxy (whatever that is) or relevance (whatever that is) may be permitted if we are committed to report the same story Peter reports in Acts: "Listen to what I have to say: Jesus of Nazareth, a man attested to you by God with deeds of power, wonders, and signs that God did through him among you, as you yourselves know—this man, handed over to you according to the definite plan and foreknowledge of God, you crucified and killed by the hands of those outside the law. But God raised him up, having freed him from death, because it was impossible for him to be held in its power" (Acts 2:22-24).

Let it be our prayer that there might still be—in an age when people are rightly interested in the gospel's social effects, intellectual implications, and emotional meaning—some people concerned to watch over "the standard of sound teaching" committed to us.

This commitment is a matter of life and death

We have not yet come to the crux of the difference between Paul's thinking and our own. It has somehow to do with the division of labor between God and ourselves or between religion and common sense. We could understand Paul as saying, "I can trust God with what I have entrusted to him," although the rhythm of the gospel song has kept us from sensing how redundant such a statement is. Or we could understand Paul as saying that God expects us to do our part. But Paul says, "I trust God that I will do my part." This seems like an illogical crossing over of two perspectives. Does not Paul weaken his sense of obligation to do his own work himself? On the other hand, does he not overestimate his own work by thinking that it is what he must trust God for? The contradiction between these criticisms should warn us that we might be thinking wrongly.

"Either God acts and we need not act, or we act and God watches from afar." Such a disbelieving disjunction sets the tone for most of our thought. We find it in New Testament scholars who label as "mythological" any mixture of what they call "this-worldly" and "otherworldly" language. We find it in the study of baptism, when it is argued that to make baptism contingent on confession of faith is to make it a human and not a divine work. We find it in the struggles of the sixteenth century, where it was argued that for people to reform church practices according to the New Testament would take the initiative away from God, whose own word properly preached will bring to pass the needed changes. We find it in ethicists, for whom responsibility for usefulness in society and culture is an alternative to discipleship. We find it in the traditional debates about faith and works: either God saves us, and we relax and trust in God, or we are responsible and must make our own plans and use our own heads.

In every case, the thinker's first concern is to disentangle divine initiative and human responsibility, this-worldly reality and otherworldly piety. No intellectual tour de force can get us across this chasm. There is no new gimmick, especially not in what some people are calling "the new theology" or "dynamic theology," to integrate anew the human and the divine. There is no way to begin with the gap and then bridge it. The only answer is to begin with the Jesus story. According to that story, divine initiative and human responsibility cannot be disentangled. They have been fused. Any theology, any pastoral technique, any social strategy that begins with God and humanity unreconciled is pre-Christian. Discipleship is social responsibility. Law is gospel. Predestination is human freedom. Faith is works. Justification is sanctification. Christ is culture. I am persuaded that God is able to keep what God has turned over to me. "Work out your own salvation with fear and trembling; for it is God who is at work in you, enabling you both to will and to work for his good pleasure" (Philippians 2:12-13).

When God became human, that human lived through real choices where his disobeying and the consequent shipwreck of the divine cause would have been possible. From the forty days in the desert to the sleepless night in the Garden of Gethsemane, the divine indwelling never protected Jesus from the real human struggle to make up his mind. For Jesus, damnation—for himself and through him for the universe—was a live option.

How could it be less the case for us than for Jesus that our eternal destiny and that of the churches in which we serve will hinge on today's faithfulness? Paul, the most accomplished of the apostles, was quite sincere about the possibility that after preaching to others he should find himself rejected (1 Corinthians 9:27). Too easily, when we hear Paul's testimony that he seeks no righteousness of his own "that comes from the law, but one that comes through faith in Christ, the righteousness from God based on faith" (Philippians 3:9), we conclude that the righteousness that counts before God is the status of having been forgiven.

Paul does not mean this. Protestantism emphasizes not righteousness achieved by my own efforts but my forgiven status before God. Paul emphasized not status before God but involvement in God's cause—involvement apart from which I would be lost. "I want to know Christ and the power of his resurrection and the sharing of his sufferings by becoming like him in his death, if somehow I may attain the resurrection from the dead" (Philippians 3:10-11).

The truly crucial difference between the apostle's worldview and our own, which makes it difficult for us to be grasped by his message, is not that, having come from a prescientific age, the Bible speaks of angels and demons, of heaven being up and hell down. The difference is that for the people of the Bible who had met God—whether this be Moses at the burning bush, Isaiah in the temple, or Paul on the Damascus Road—God's will had become without question and without rival the overwhelming passion of their lives. But today that passion is out of style. It betrays, we fear, a lack of perspective. It reminds us of the sometimes brittle, sometimes brutal compulsiveness which the legends of our age associate with the puritan and the fanatic. Today we fear not damnation but one-sidedness, not lukewarmness but intolerance. The only thing we can respectably be compulsive about in our generation is recreation. The only thing we can be enthusiastic about is the therapeutic approach.

Our real need is neither to rediscover the Anabaptist vision nor to discover new dimensions in ecumenical theology, seminary curriculum, or congregational management. We need to be discovered, uncovered, touched by the finger of God behind the last-ditch defenses of our relaxedness. We need to be shaken with the awareness that not only the world, but we ourselves and the lukewarm church we have come to accept as normal, stand before the real possibility of ultimate rejection by the one whom we have been calling, "Lord, Lord" (Matthew 7:22-23).

Let this be our third lesson. The divine indwelling of our life means more, not less, earnestness about the size of our task. The message of reconciliation and pardon means more, not less, willingness to trust that the Lord will work things out. It means that more, not less, depends on whether there truly comes to birth in our families, in our studies, and in our congregations a new fellowship of personalities that have been broken in to the divine harness and liberated for conformity to the image of God's blessed Son.

Let it be our prayer that we might place no more obstacles—not even the obstacle of our own realistic humility—in the way of God's working in us both to will and to do all that God has assigned to us.

Our commitment is the way of the cross

The reason Paul wrote this passage is his fear that Timothy might be "ashamed" because of the suffering their calling involved for both of them. The "standard of sound teaching" that constitutes the apostolic "deposit" centers in the dying love of the Lord. The obedience on which our salvation depends or, more precisely, in which our salvation becomes a reality, is to carry around in our bodies the dying of Jesus, so that in our bodies the life of Jesus may be revealed (2 Corinthians 4:10). To follow Christ means doctrine and piety, worship and church order, mission methods and healing the sick. But first of all it means living the cross. The plea to Timothy expands into a hymn of confidence that God is able. That hymn of confidence soon comes to earth in the reminder, "You are aware that all who are in Asia have turned away from me" (2 Timothy 1:15).

Paul, the trained thinker and zealous Pharisee, is brought by God to preaching folly and a stumbling block. Paul, the world traveler, wastes away in his prison. Paul, the church leader and great missionary strategist, is deserted by his colleagues. For us it is not much of a feat to be fools or a stumbling block, but until our faithfulness gives us some taste of chains and of desertion, of being hobbled by the world and disowned by the church, we shall not understand the depth of the divine condescension or the majesty of the triumph of our Lord, whose power is made perfect in weakness (2 Corinthians 12:9). The cross of Christ and the cross of the Christian are not some senseless suffering one must simply endure, but rather the wisdom and the power of God.

The faithfulness of ministers of the gospel, whether those the world calls ministers or those the world calls laity, will ultimately be tested not by their expertness, speech, thought, or counseling, but by the moral challenge of facing evil in the world, whether this be the evil of hunger, of sickness in body and spirit, of hostility among people and groups of people, of appetite, or of unbelief.

We have already triumphed over the world, but the path which that triumph takes—from the day it was made sure until the day it shall be made manifest—is the way of the cross.

The Author

John Howard Yoder (1927–1997) taught ethics and theology at Notre Dame University and Associated Mennonite Biblical Seminary. He received his doctorate from the University of Basel, Switzerland, and was a member of Prairie Street Mennonite Church in Elkhart, Indiana. Widely recognized around the world as a theological educator, ethicist, and interpreter of biblical pacifism, he is best known for his seminal book *The Politics of Jesus*.

The Editors

John C. Nugent (PhD, Calvin Theological Seminary) is professor of Old Testament at Great Lakes Christian College in Lansing, Michigan. He is the author of *The Politics of Yahweh* (Cascade Books, 2011) and the editor of *The End of Sacrifice* (Herald Press, 2011) and *Radical Ecumenicity* (ACU Press, 2010). He has published articles in books, academic journals, and popular-level magazines. He also heads up the John Howard Yoder Indexing Project, serves as a consulting editor for the *Stone-Campbell Journal*, and writes Bible lesson commentaries for Standard Publishing.

Andy Alexis-Baker is currently a PhD candidate in systematic theology and theological ethics at Marquette University. He has published numerous articles in academic journals, including *Scottish Journal of Theology*, *Journal of Church and State*, *Biblical Interpretation*, *Mennonite Quarterly Review*, and *Journal of Early Christian Studies*. He is the coeditor of John Howard Yoder's *Christian Attitudes to War, Peace, and Revolution* (Brazos, 2009) and Yoder's forthcoming *Theology of Missions* (IVP Academic, 2013), as well as the co–general editor of the Peaceable Kingdom Series with Cascade Books.

Branson L. Parler (PhD, Calvin Theological Seminary) is associate professor of theological studies at Kuyper College in Grand Rapids, Michigan. He has previously published articles on John Howard Yoder and, with John Nugent and Jason Vance, has developed an online searchable index of the works of John Howard Yoder (www.yoderindex.com). He is the author of *Things Hold Together: John Howard Yoder's Trinitarian Theology of Culture* (Herald Press, 2012).